KU-255-518

ANGOLA

ARMS TRADE AND VIOLATIONS OF THE LAWS OF WAR SINCE THE 1992 ELECTIONS

Sumário em Portugués

**Human Rights Watch Arms Project
and
Human Rights Watch/Africa
(formerly Africa Watch)**

**Human Rights Watch
New York•Washington•Los Angeles•London•Brussels**

Copyright © November 1994 by Human Rights Watch
All rights reserved.
Printed in the United States of America.

Library of Congress Catalog Card Number: 94-79743
ISBN: 1-56432-145-2

Human Rights Watch Arms Project
Human Rights Watch's Arms Project was established in 1992 to monitor and prevent arms transfers to governments or organizations grossly violating internationally recognized human rights and the laws of war and promote freedom of information regarding arms transfers worldwide. Joost R. Hiltermann is the director, Stephen D. Goose is the program director; Kathleen A. Bleakley is the associate.

Human Rights Watch/Africa (formerly Africa Watch)
Human Rights Watch's Africa division was established in 1988 to monitor and promote the observance of internationally recognized human rights in Africa. Abdullahi An-Na'im is the executive director; Janet Fleischman is the Washington representative; Karen Sorensen, Alex Vines and Berhane Woldegabriel are research associates; Kimberly Mazyck and Urmi Shah are associates; Bronwen Manby is a consultant. William Carmichael is the chair of the advisory committee and Alice Brown is the vice chair.

HUMAN RIGHTS WATCH

Human Rights Watch conducts regular, systematic investigations of human rights at some seventy countries around the world. It addresses the human rights pract governments of all political stripes, of all geopolitical alignments, and of all ethn religious persuasions. In internal wars it documents violations by both governmen rebel groups. Human Rights Watch defends freedom of thought and expression, due p and equal protection of the law; it documents and denounces murders, disappeara torture, arbitrary imprisonment, exile, censorship and other abuses of internatio recognized human rights.

Human Rights Watch began in 1978 with the founding of its Helsinki divis Today, it includes five divisions covering Africa, the Americas, Asia, the Middle East well as the signatories of the Helsinki accords. It also includes five collaborative proje on arms transfers, children's rights, free expression, prison conditions, and women's righ It maintains offices in New York, Washington, Los Angeles, London, Brussels, Mosco Belgrade, Zagreb, Dushanbe, and Hong Kong. Human Rights Watch is an independen nongovernmental organization, supported by contributions from private individuals an foundations worldwide. It accepts no government funds, directly or indirectly.

The staff includes Kenneth Roth, executive director; Cynthia Brown, program director; Holly J. Burkhalter, advocacy director; Gara LaMarche, associate director; Juan Méndez, general counsel; Susan Osnos, communications director; and Derrick Wong, finance and administration director.

The regional directors of Human Rights Watch are Abdullahi An-Na'im, Africa; José Miguel Vivanco, Americas; Sidney Jones, Asia; Jeri Laber, Helsinki; and Christopher E. George, Middle East. The project directors are Stephen Goose (acting), Arms Project; Lois Whitman, Children's Rights Project; Gara LaMarche, Free Expression Project; Joanna Weschler, Prison Project; and Dorothy Q. Thomas, Women's Rights Project.

The members of the board of directors are Robert L. Bernstein, chair; Adrian W. DeWind, vice chair; Roland Algrant, Lisa Anderson, Peter D. Bell, Alice L. Brown, William Carmichael, Dorothy Cullman, Irene Diamond, Edith Everett, Jonathan Fanton, Alan Finberg, Jack Greenberg, Alice H. Henkin, Harold Hongju Koh, Stephen L. Kass, Marina Pinto Kaufman, Alexander MacGregor, Josh Mailman, Peter Osnos, Kathleen Peratis, Bruce Rabb, Orville Schell, Gary G. Sick, Malcolm Smith, Nahid Toubia, Maureen White, and Rosalind C. Whitehead.

Addresses for Human Rights Watch
485 Fifth Avenue, New York, NY 10017-6104
Tel: (212) 972-8400, Fax: (212) 972-0905. E-mail: hrwatchnyc@igc.apc.org

1522 K Street, N.W., #910, Washington, DC 20005-1202
Tel: (202) 371-6592, Fax: (202) 371-0124. E-mail: hrwatchdc@igc.apc.org

10951 West Pico Blvd., #203, Los Angeles, CA 90064-2126
Tel: (310) 475-3070, Fax: (310) 475-5613. E-mail: hrwatchla@igc.apc.org

33 Islington High Street, N1 9LH London, UK
Tel: (71) 713-1995, Fax: (71) 713-1800, E-mail: hrwatchuk@gn.apc.org

15 Rue Van Campenhout, 1040 Brussels, Belgium
Tel: (2) 732-2009, Fax: (2) 732-0471, E-mail: hrwatcheu@gn.apc.org

CONTENTS

ACKNOWLEDGMENTS ix
GLOSSARY x
I. SUMMARY 1
    KEY RECOMMENDATIONS 5
II. BACKGROUND 8
    THE 1992 ELECTIONS 10
        MPLA Campaign 10
        UNITA Campaign 11
        Election Results 12
    THE FAILED DEMOBILIZATION 12
        MPLA Non-Cooperation 13
        UNITA Delays 14
        United Nations Ineffectiveness 15
    THE POST-ELECTION CRISIS: SAVIMBI REJECTS
    RESULTS 17
    WAR RETURNS TO ANGOLA 18
        UNITA Offensive and Government Response 18
        Government Counter-Offensive 19
        UNITA Gains in 1993 20
        Tide Turns Again 21
III. MILITARY ORGANIZATION, STRUCTURE, AND
    OPERATIONS 23
    UNITA 23
        Pre-Election Military 23
        Current Operations 24
    GOVERNMENT FORCES 25
        Ground Forces 26
            Northern Front 27
                Luanda 27
                Soyo and Cabinda 27
            Northeastern Front—Central Malanje
            Province 28
            Central Front 28
                Cuanza Sul Province 28
                Benguela 28
            Southern Front—Northern
            Namibe/Lubango 28

Special Forces 29
The Air Force 29
FOREIGN SECURITY PERSONNEL AND EXECUTIVE
OUTCOMES 30
IV. ARMS PROCUREMENT 35
THE GOVERNMENT 35
The Nora Heeren 37
Africa's Number One Arms Buyer 38
Arms Suppliers 39
Russia 39
Brazil 41
North Korea 42
Portugal 42
Spain 44
Other Nations 45
UNITA 47
Sanction-Busting 48
Arming UNITA 49
Zaire: Diamonds, Arms, Bases, Troops 49
South Africa 51
Namibia 54
Russia 55
United Kingdom 56
Other Nations 57
Diamonds for Arms Deals 57
TRANSPARENCY IN ARMS TRANSFERS 59
V. VIOLATIONS OF THE LAWS OF WAR BY GOVERNMENT
FORCES 61
THE PURGE OF THE CITIES—OCTOBER 1992-
JANUARY 1993 61
Luanda 61
Lubango 70
Lobito and Benguela 72
Other Cities 73
CONTINUING ABUSES IN 1993 AND 1994 74
Quilengues—Summary Executions On the Front
Line 74
Huambo—Bombs, Mines, Children, and Human
Shields 75

Kuito—Killing for Food 76
Malanje—Cutting Off the Hands of Children 76
INDISCRIMINATE BOMBING AND SHELLING 77
Applicable Legal Standards 82
TORTURE AND MISTREATMENT OF PRISONERS 83
FORCED DISPLACEMENT 84
CHILD SOLDIERS 85
VI. VIOLATIONS OF THE LAWS OF WAR BY UNITA
FORCES 88
THE CITY SIEGES 89
Huambo 89
Retreat   from   Huambo—Summary
Executions 90
Semana de Loucura (Crazy Week) 90
Underage Recruitment 93
Kuito 93
Shelling 94
Sniper Fire 98
Starvation of Civilians 99
Divided families 100
Malanje 100
Landmines 101
STARVATION AS A METHOD OF COMBAT 102
HUMANITARIAN ASSISTANCE 104
UNITA OUTSIDE THE MAIN TOWNS 106
Summary Executions 106
Forced Portering 107
"Taxation" of Food 108
Mistreatment of Government Soldiers 109
Wanton Brutality 109
UNDERAGE RECRUITMENT 112
SLAVE-LIKE CONDITIONS 112
SOBAS 115
PRISONERS 115
HOSTAGES 116
INDISCRIMINATE LAYING OF MINES 118
VII.   THE   U.N.   AND   INTERNATIONAL   MEDIATION
ATTEMPTS 122
AFTER THE ELECTIONS 122

NAMIBE TALKS 123
ADDIS ABABA TALKS 124
ABIDJAN TALKS 125
LUSAKA TALKS 129
U.S. POLICY 132
VIII. APPLICATION OF THE LAWS OF WAR TO THE
       ANGOLAN CONFLICT 134
       A NEW NON-INTERNATIONAL ARMED CONFLICT . . . 134
       THE APPLICATION OF ARTICLE 3 135
       CUSTOMARY INTERNATIONAL LAW APPLICABLE TO
            INTERNAL ARMED CONFLICTS 137
       PROTECTION OF THE CIVILIAN POPULATION UNDER
            THE RULES OF WAR 138
       DESIGNATION OF MILITARY OBJECTIVES 139
       PROHIBITED ACTS 140
       TAXATION OR FOOD REQUISITION 141
       PROHIBITION ON INDISCRIMINATE ATTACKS: THE
            PRINCIPLE OF PROPORTIONALITY 142
       PROTECTION OF CIVILIANS FROM DISPLACEMENT
            FOR REASONS RELATED TO THE CONFLICT . . 144
       STARVATION OF CIVILIANS AS A METHOD OF
            COMBAT 145
            Proof of Intention to Starve Civilians 147
       SIEGES 148
       RECRUITMENT OF CHILD SOLDIERS 150
IX. RECOMMENDATIONS 153
            Angolan Government 153
            UNITA 153
            United Nations 154
            The Observing Troika (Portugal, Russia, United
                 States) 155
            South African, Zairian, and Other Governments in
                 the Region 156
APPENDIX: SUMÁRIO EM PORTUGUÉS 157
       PRINCIPAIS RECOMENDAÇÕES 162

ACKNOWLEDGMENTS

The research and writing for this report was done by Alex Vines, a research associate for Human Rights Watch/Africa. The report is based primarily on his fieldwork in Angola, Zambia, South Africa, and Zimbabwe in May and June 1994 for the Human Rights Watch Arms Project and Human Rights Watch/Africa. Additional material was gathered during his trip to South Africa and Mozambique in September 1994. The report also draws upon material from a visit to Angola by Mr. Vines during the September/October 1992 election period. Chapter Eight on the rules of war was written by Jemera Rone, counsel to Human Rights Watch. The report was edited by Stephen Goose, program director of the Arms Project. Kathleen Bleakley, Arms Project associate, provided research assistance and prepared the report for publication. Luisa Handem, a former HRW/Africa associate, translated the summary into Portuguese.

Human Rights Watch would like to acknowledge with thanks the informed comments of: Dame Margaret Anstee, the former U.N. Special Representative in Angola; Shawn McCormick of the Center for Strategic and International Studies in Washington, D.C.; Karl Maier of the *Independent* newspaper; Nicholas Shaxson of *Reuters* in Luanda; Gillian Nevins of Amnesty International; Christine Messiant of the Centre D'Etudes Africaines, L'Ecole des Hautes Etudes en Sciences Sociales in Paris; and, Mercedes Sayagues, Information Officer for the U.N. World Food Program in Harare.

Human Rights Watch is grateful to Sarah Longford and the U.N. Humanitarian Coordination Unit in Luanda for facilitating air transportation to Huambo and Kuito. Human Rights Watch thanks the London-based Economist Intelligence Unit (EIU) for its donation of a copy of *Angola to 2000: prospects for recovery*, by Tony Hodges. We are grateful for the assistance of many others who have asked to remain anonymous.

The Arms Project acknowledges with appreciation funding from the Rockefeller Foundation, New York.

GLOSSARY

CNE   National Electoral Council

EO   Executive Outcomes — a South African firm, accused by UNITA of providing mercenary support to the Angolan government.

FAA   Forças Armadas Angolanas (Angolan Armed Forces) — the new, post-election military of the Angolan government.

FALA   Forças Armadas de Libertação de Angola — UNITA's army.

FAPLA   Forças Armadas para a Libertação de Angola — the Angolan government's old, pre-election armed forces.

FNLA   Frente Nacional de Libertação de Angola — one of the three nationalist groups that fought for independence.

ICRC   International Committee of the Red Cross

MPLA   Movimento Popular de Libertação de Angola (Popular Movement for the Liberation of Angola) — the MPLA is now the governing party of the government of Angola; it was one of the three nationalist groups that fought for independence and then militarily defeated the other two groups.

NGO   Non-governmental organization

OAU   Organization of African Unity

SADF   South African Defense Forces

UCAH   U.N. Humanitarian Assistance Coordination Unit

UNAVEM   United Nations Angola Verification Mission

UNITA   União Nacional para a Independência Total de Angola
               (National Union for the Total Independence of Angola) —
               the opposition guerrilla force in Angola.

WFP   U.N. World Food Program

I. SUMMARY

Angola returned to civil war within one month of its first nationwide elections, held in September 1992. The human cost since fighting resumed is impossible to determine with precision, but the United Nations estimates that more than 100,000 have died. The U.N. reported that as many as 1,000 people were dying daily from conflict, starvation, and disease in mid-1993—more than in any other conflict in the world at that time. In October 1993, 250 child deaths were reported each day in the besieged government-held city of Malanje alone.[1] In September 1994, the U.N. Secretary-General reported that there had been a ten percent increase in the number of people severely affected by the war since February 1994, and that nearly 3.7 million Angolans, mostly displaced and conflict-affected, were in need of emergency supplies, including essential medicines, vaccines and food aid.[2]

In addition to the appalling levels of death and destruction, this war is notable for widespread and systematic violations of the laws of war by both the government and the rebels—the União Nacional para a Independência Total de Angola (UNITA). In particular, indiscriminate shelling of starving, besieged cities by UNITA has resulted in massive destruction of property and the loss of untold numbers of civilian lives. Indiscriminate bombing by the government has also taken a high civilian toll. As noted by an Africa expert from the U.S. Department of Defense, "This type of warfare bears mainly, cruelly and disproportionately on the populace, which is caught between the warring

---

[1] Child deaths reportedly had decreased to twenty-six per day by January 1994. See, *Angola in Strife*, Situation Report No. 6, U.S. Agency for International Development, April 7, 1994.

[2] United Nations Security Council, S/1994/1069, "Report of the Secretary-General on the United Nations Angola Verification Mission," September 1994.

parties."[3] If the human cost is staggering, so is the lack of international attention. Angola has earned the sobriquet of "the forgotten war."

This report documents the violations of the laws of war, and the influx of weaponry feeding those violations in Angola since the elections in 1992. The elections were the culmination of a flawed peace agreement, known as the Bicesse Accords, signed in Portugal on May 31, 1991 by the government and UNITA. The accords contained a so-called "Triple Zero" clause which prohibited either side from acquiring new supplies of weapons. During the transition period leading up to the September 1992 elections, the government and UNITA failed to abide by their obligation to demobilize soldiers. Instead, both apparently maintained secret armies, and the government created a new paramilitary police force, known as the "Ninjas." The United Nations, with a limited mandate and grossly inadequate resources, was ineffectual during this period, and was virtually silent on human rights abuses.

When the ruling party of the government—the Movimento Popular de Libertação de Angola (MPLA)—won the elections, UNITA rejected the results and launched a military offensive. This quickly escalated into a return to full-scale civil war, and fighting remains intense to this day.

The renewed conflict, and accompanying human rights abuses and violations of laws of war, are being fueled by new flows of arms into the country. There is evidence of arms shipments to the government in 1991 and 1992 in violation of the Bicesse Accords, notably from Russia and Brazil. When war resumed in Angola, the government revoked the Triple Zero arms embargo, and went on an international arms shopping spree, buying more than $3.5 billion worth of weapons in 1993 and 1994. Weapons procurement has reached record levels, surpassing even the extraordinary years of the mid-1980s when the Soviet Union was pumping arms into Angola as its part of a superpower proxy war. The government of Angola has unquestionably been the largest arms purchaser in sub-Saharan Africa during the past two years. The government appears to be undermining its economic future through massive arms imports. Some analysts believe that Angola has mortgaged the next seven years of oil production to

---

[3] James Woods, Deputy Assistant Secretary of Defense for African Affairs, in "The Quest for Peace in Angola," Hearing before the Subcommittee on Africa of the House Foreign Affairs Committee, (Washington: U.S. Government Printing Office), November 16, 1993, p. 7. Mr. Woods estimated that military casualties totalled "only a few thousand over the past year," while civilian deaths could be as high as half a million. Ibid.

finance arms buys, even though its current oil reserves are estimated to last only fifteen years.

The government is continuing to purchase a full range of weaponry, from small arms and ammunition to tanks and aircraft, including some advanced systems not seen before in Angola, such as the T-72 tank. The government is buying weapons from numerous sources, including governments in Europe, Africa, Asia, and Latin America, although much of the weaponry is purchased from private international arms dealers. Most of the arms deals are cloaked in secrecy and subterfuge; many involve false documentation. Many involve multiple governmental and private actors. Russia appears to have inherited from the former Soviet Union the distinction of being the largest arms supplier to Angola. Other nations apparently involved in arming the government include Brazil, Ukraine, Bulgaria, Uzbekistan, North Korea, Portugal, and Spain. Portugal and Russia have acted irresponsibly in undermining their role as members of the official "Observing Troika" for the peace process.

A private South African "security consultant" firm, Executive Outcomes, has apparently provided armed personnel to assist both UNITA and government forces, and currently has a multi-million dollar contract with the Angolan government.

UNITA is purchasing large amounts of weaponry from foreign sources, as well. Such purchases violate both the 1991 Bicesse Accords and the international arms and oil embargo against UNITA imposed by the United Nations Security Council in September 1993. UNITA has been effective in "sanctions-busting" through neighboring countries, especially South Africa, Namibia, and Zaire. UNITA appears to obtain much of its weaponry from private sources, rather than foreign governments, although there is some evidence that Russia, Zaire, and others have provided arms. Zaire has become the most important source of support for UNITA. UNITA uses Zaire as a transit area and conduit for diamond sales and weapons transfers, maintains a number of small rear bases in Zaire, and receives operational support from Zairian troops.

UNITA is financing its military campaign, including illegal arms imports, with Angola's diamond wealth. The De Beers diamond cartel and other international dealers are buying diamonds mined in violation of Angolan law in UNITA-held territory. Most of the diamonds are smuggled across Zaire's southern border, and, to a lesser extent, the Zambian border. De Beers admits spending $500 million to buy legally and illegally mined diamonds from Angola in 1992. Money from the diamond trade is replacing assistance UNITA previously received from the United States and South Africa. U.S. covert aid to UNITA totalled about $250 million between 1986 and 1991.

The Angolan government has been responsible for widespread human rights abuses and violations of the rules of war since the September 1992 elections, including:

- indiscriminate aerial bombardment of population centers;
- use of torture, disappearance, and summary execution, particularly against suspected UNITA supporters in the urban areas;
- the killing of civilians and pillaging during military operations;
- restrictions on relief operations by international and U.N. agencies, and impunity given to army officers and others who profiteer on relief food;
- recruitment of child soldiers and other arbitrary recruitment;
- forced recruitment of foreign nationals under U.N. protection into military service;
- forced displacement of the civilian population; and,
- cruel and inhuman prison conditions.

Government forces, and civilian groups armed by the government, tortured and killed thousands of suspected UNITA supporters—civilian non-combatants—between October 1992 and January 1993 in a purge of the cities after the war resumed. Thousands more civilians have been killed or injured in the indiscriminate bombing of population centers in UNITA-controlled zones during 1993 and 1994.

UNITA has also committed systematic and horrendous violations of the laws of war since the September 1992 elections, including:

- indiscriminate shelling of besieged cities;
- summary execution and torture;
- attempts to starve civilians by attacking international relief operations, mining footpaths and fields, sabotaging road transportation, and capturing or killing those tending their fields;
- mutilation of the dead;
- abduction of civilians, including women and children, and sometimes treating them like slaves;
- recruitment of child soldiers and other arbitrary recruitment, and denying unaccompanied minors the opportunity to be voluntarily reunited with their families;
- taking foreign nationals as hostages, including using them as "human shields;"

• restriction of the movements of civilians in areas it occupies, confiscating food from them and forcing them to do unpaid labor; and,
• cruel and inhuman prison conditions.

UNITA has laid siege to a number of cities and towns, most notably Huambo and Kuito. UNITA rained as many as 1,000 shells per day on both cities. An estimated 10,000 people died in the battle for Huambo, many of them civilians. After capturing Huambo, UNITA slaughtered many civilians on the roads exiting the city, and many of the civilians who remained behind. It is believed that 20-30,000 people died in the twenty-one month siege of Kuito that completely devastated the city. UNITA sieges have caused widespread starvation of the civilian population, especially in Kuito and Malanje. UNITA attacks on humanitarian relief operations are numerous and well-documented.

Mine warfare has intensified since hostilities resumed, with thousands of new mines being laid by both the government and UNITA to obstruct roads and bridges, to encircle besieged towns with mine belts up to three kilometers wide, and to despoil agricultural lands. There are an estimated nine to fifteen million mines laid throughout the country. The U.N. has estimated that the number of mine amputees in Angola will reach 70,000 in 1994.

U.N. and other mediation efforts have been undermined often by intransigence on the part of both UNITA and the government, and by attempts by both sides to use the negotiations for battlefield advantage. Despite granting official recognition of the Angolan government, U.S. policy under the Clinton administration has changed little from U.S. policy at the end of the Bush administration: substituting political initiatives aimed at furthering the peace process for the previous policy of arming UNITA. Angola appears to be a low foreign policy priority for the U.S. The Clinton administration largely has kept silent about human rights abuses and violations of the laws of war in Angola.

KEY RECOMMENDATIONS

Human Rights Watch calls on the Angolan government to respect international humanitarian and human rights law, particularly the prohibitions on targeting civilians, indiscriminate bombardment, and destruction or looting of civilian property. The government should stop using weapons especially harmful to the civilian population, such as antipersonnel landmines and cluster bombs. The government should forbid summary executions and torture, and punish those responsible for such acts. The government should halt the seizure by troops and officials of food and non-food items from the civilian population that expose civilians to the threat of death through starvation, disease, or exposure. The government should stop the use of child soldiers and involuntary recruitment. The government should permit the International Committee of the Red Cross to visit persons detained in connection with the conflict.

Human Rights Watch calls on UNITA to respect international humanitarian law, particularly prohibitions on targeting civilians, indiscriminate bombardment, and destruction or looting of civilian property. UNITA should immediately cease using starvation as a method of combat, and stop indiscriminately shelling cities and attacking humanitarian relief operations. UNITA should stop using weapons especially harmful to the civilian population, such as antipersonnel landmines. UNITA should forbid summary executions and torture, and punish those responsible for such acts. UNITA should stop the use of child soldiers, involuntary recruitment, and forced portering. UNITA should permit freedom of movement and facilitate voluntary family reunification. UNITA should halt the seizure by soldiers and officials of food and non-food items from the civilian population that expose civilians to the threat of death through starvation, disease, or exposure. UNITA should permit the International Committee of the Red Cross to visit persons detained in connection with the conflict. UNITA should cooperate with relief efforts and human rights monitors and educators, and facilitate their access to all parts of the country.

Human Rights Watch recommends that the U.N. Security Council institute an arms embargo on Angola, applicable to both the government and UNITA. Member states should submit all information on past weapons exports to Angola to the U.N. Register on Conventional Arms. The U.N. should deploy full-time U.N. monitors at Zaire's Ndjili international airport to tighten U.N. sanctions against UNITA. The U.N. should authorize a contingent of full-time U.N. human rights monitors to observe, investigate, bring to the attention of responsible authorities, and make public human rights abuses and violations of humanitarian laws by all parties. The monitors should have access to all parts of Angola and some should be based in locations well-placed for access to the changing fronts of the conflict.

The U.N. should draft a ceasefire agreement so that its terms do not reward military aggression and violations of the laws of war since the breaking of the Bicesse Accords. Human rights must be protected under the terms of the agreement. Once a peace agreement is signed, the U.N. should expand the deployment of human rights monitors and launch a civilian-directed and -staffed program of human rights education across the country irrespective of party, creed or ethnic origin.

Human Rights Watch recommends that Portugal, Russia and the United States, as official mediators in the peace process, should impose immediate national arms embargoes, and make public details on any weapons sales or other military assistance to either combatant party in Angola since the signing of the Bicesse Accords in 1991. These observers should maintain pressure on the Angolan government and particularly UNITA to respect human rights and humanitarian law and permit access to relief operations. These nations should support the creation of a full-time U.N. human rights monitoring team.

Human Rights Watch calls on the South African, Zairian, and other regional governments to assist the U.N. in its attempts to monitor and prevent UNITA sanction-busting. These governments should prohibit any mercenary support which contributes to violations of the laws of war. The government of Zaire should take all measures to stop the use of Zaire as a conduit for illegal arms trade, and should not allow UNITA to maintain rear bases in Zairian border areas.

II. BACKGROUND

War has raged in Angola for two decades, except for the period between May 1991, when a ceasefire was signed, and September 1992, when the first national elections were held.[1] The conflict began in 1975 when three nationalist groups that had been fighting against Portuguese colonial rule--the MPLA, UNITA and the Frente Nacional de Libertação de Angola (FNLA)--battled each other to occupy Luanda by November 11, the official date for independence. The Soviet Union and Cuba supported the MPLA, which controlled Luanda but little else. South Africa invaded Angola in support of UNITA. Zaire invaded in support of the FNLA. The United States provided extensive assistance to both UNITA and the FNLA. In October, a massive Soviet airlift of arms and Cuban troops turned the tide in favor of the MPLA. South African and Zairian troops withdrew, and the MPLA was able to form a single party socialist government which obtained widespread diplomatic recognition, though not from the U.S. or South Africa.

UNITA and FNLA then joined forces against the MPLA. Although UNITA was initially driven out of its Huambo headquarters and its forces scattered and driven into the bush, UNITA regrouped and waged a devastating, long-running war against the MPLA government, which it saw as *assimilado* (very urban, educated and Portuguese-oriented), mestizo (mixed race), and northern-dominated. UNITA portrayed itself as anti-Marxist and pro-Western, but it had its own regional roots, primarily amongst the Ovimbundu of southern and central Angola.

The war spread, with UNITA making steady gains. South African forces intermittently operated in Angola in support of UNITA. The largest South African incursions occurred in 1981-83, in part as retaliation for MPLA support for the South West African People's Organization's guerrilla war against South African-occupied Namibia. During this period, South African forces occupied parts of the extreme south of Angola.

In late 1983, the U.N. Security Council demanded South African withdrawal from Angola. Shortly afterwards, the two countries signed the Lusaka Accords under which South Africa agreed to withdraw if Angola ceased

---

[1] Previous Human Rights Watch reports on Angola include: Africa Watch, *Landmines in Angola* (New York: Human Rights Watch, 1993); Africa Watch, "Angola: Civilians Devastated by 15-Year War," February 1991; and, Africa Watch, *Angola: Violations of the Laws of War by Both Sides* (New York: Human Rights Watch, 1989).

its support for SWAPO. However, in 1985 South Africa launched another invasion to counter a major government offensive against UNITA, carried out with the assistance of some 50,000 Cuban troops.

U.S. covert assistance to UNITA, which had been prohibited by the U.S. Congress (the Clark Amendment) in 1976, was resumed after the repeal of the amendment in 1985. U.S. covert aid totalled about $250 million between 1986 and 1991, making it the second largest U.S. covert program, exceeded only by aid to the Afghan mujahidin.

By 1987, there were major battles in the south of Angola, culminating in the siege of Cuito Cuanavale by South African and UNITA forces. Although the fighting over Cuito Cuanavale resulted in a military stalemate, the outcome was a psychological defeat for the South African Defense Forces (SADF), which came to believe that it could not win militarily in Angola. This prompted a significant re-thinking of South African military strategy.

Cuito Cuanavale also marked the beginning of new diplomatic attempts to end the conflict. In 1988, the Soviet Union signalled that it was no longer prepared to arm the MPLA indefinitely. In January 1989, President dos Santos made an offer to Jonas Savimbi which led to a peace process brokered by eighteen African nations. At a meeting in Gbadolite, Zaire, on June 22, 1989, Dos Santos and Savimbi shook hands and agreed on an immediate ceasefire. But it quickly collapsed, as a dispute developed over what was agreed to orally and especially over what Savimbi's future role would be.

The following eighteen months saw simultaneously the most sustained efforts to achieve a peaceful settlement and some of the fiercest fighting of the entire war. Between April 1990 and May 1991 six rounds of talks took place between UNITA and the government.[2] The negotiations were hosted by Portugal, with observers from the U.S. and the Soviet Union; these nations were subsequently called the Observing Troika. In May 1991 the talks resulted in an agreement known as the Bicesse Accords, which temporarily ended a conflict that had already left between 100,000 and 350,000 battle dead. The agreement was made possible in part by the ending of the Cold War, which facilitated U.S.-Soviet cooperation, and the desire of the Soviet Union and Cuba to reduce their considerable financial commitment to Angola.

---

[2] Moisés Venâncio and Carla McMillan, "Portuguese Mediation of the Angola Conflict in 1990-1," in Stephen Chan and Vivienne Jabri (eds.), *Mediation in Southern Africa* (London: MacMillan, 1993); Abiodun Williams, "Negotiations and the End of the Angolan Civil War," in David Smock (ed.), *Making War and Waging Peace: Foreign Intervention in Africa* (Washington, DC: U.S. Institute of Peace Press, 1993).

The accords ratified a ceasefire and called for government and UNITA forces to be integrated into a 50,000-strong military force, the *Forças Armadas Angolanas* (FAA). The accords contained a so-called "Triple Zero" clause which prohibited either side from purchasing new supplies of weaponry.[3] Under the accords, the MPLA remained the legitimate and internationally-recognized government, retaining responsibility for running the state during the interim period and for setting the date of elections.

THE 1992 ELECTIONS

In November 1991 President José Eduardo dos Santos announced that legislative and presidential elections would be held in September 1992.

MPLA Campaign

By April 1991, the MPLA had moved a long way from its Marxist-Leninist roots and was adopting a free-market economy. Still, many observers expected the MPLA to collapse in the interval between the ceasefire and the elections. Indeed, in mid-1992 even many MPLA officials believed that their party would be defeated in the elections because of the electorate's desire for change after years of single-party rule, and also because of the party's corrupt reputation. In June 1992 Western intelligence claimed to have exposed a plot by senior members of the MPLA to assassinate Savimbi, and Britain reportedly sent a Special Air Services (SAS) unit to protect him in an attempt to ensure that the peace process was not derailed.

Even in MPLA strongholds, such as the city of Malanje, the government was not fully confident of its chances. In September 1992 government special forces units (known as FUBU) were transferred to Malanje under the supervision of Governor João Bernardo (a former intelligence chief) to prevent UNITA's armed forces from infiltrating the city. The FUBU units were under orders to encourage anti-U.N. sentiment and to depict it as pro-UNITA. If the MPLA fared badly in the elections it intended to blame the U.N. for helping UNITA. The FUBU would shout anti-U.N. slogans during the day and fire gunshots at night, mostly in the direction of areas in which UNITA

---

[3] The clause states: "The cease-fire agreement will oblige the parties to cease receiving lethal material. The United States, the Union of Soviet Socialist Republics, and all other countries will support the implementation of the cease-fire and will refrain from furnishing lethal material to any of the Angolan parties."

supporters were concentrated, but also toward the U.N. compound. In the end, the MPLA won in Malanje.

The MPLA also created the "Emergency Police"—a highly trained, armed paramilitary unit, popularly known as the "Ninjas." Originally 4,000 strong, the Emergency Police was filled with elite troops from the regular army and government security forces, in contravention of the Bicesse agreements. The Ninjas demonstrated their military effectiveness in late October 1992 when they operated against UNITA in Luanda. As the government's premier fighting unit, the Ninjas have subsequently been engaged in combat against UNITA across the country, and their ranks have swollen to some 10-20,000. They are now officially known as the Rapid Intervention Police.

Aside from these heavy-handed measures, the government mounted an effective and sophisticated publicity campaign, using the expertise of the Brazilian public relations company that had facilitated victory for former Brazilian President Collor de Mello.

UNITA Campaign

Jonas Savimbi has dominated UNITA since its formation in 1966. Savimbi's charisma and strong leadership were thought to be an electoral asset, especially in rural areas. A human rights scandal in mid-1992 over UNITA's execution in late 1991 of two of its senior officials, Wilson dos Santos and Tito Chingunji, was paradoxically believed by some Angolans to have strengthened Savimbi's electoral chances by emphasizing that he was a strong man.

Until June 1992, all the main Western assessments continued to forecast that Savimbi was likely to win the presidential elections, although graffiti seen on walls in several towns pointed to popular ambivalence: "UNITA kills, MPLA steals." But, by September the tide had turned away from UNITA. The government's publicity campaign contributed to this shift, as did the content of Savimbi's speeches, including anti-white and anti-mestizo rhetoric, and UNITA's arrogant behavior in the cities, such as setting up roadblocks with impunity. In his final campaign speeches Savimbi frightened many urban voters by saying that UNITA would purge state sector employees suspected of having supported the MPLA in the past. Because many Angolans are dependent on state employment for their survival, this seems to have convinced many undecided urban voters not to risk voting for Savimbi. As one high ranking government official said to Human Rights Watch in May 1994: "We didn't win those elections. Savimbi lost them."

Election Results

Held on the last two days of September 1992, the elections provided the first opportunity for Angolans to express their political will in what the U.N. and other foreign observers concluded was a "generally free and fair" process. With a turnout of over 91 percent (4.4 million) of registered voters, President dos Santos received 49.6 percent of the vote against 40 percent for Jonas Savimbi. In the legislative election, the MPLA obtained 54 percent of the vote against UNITA's 34 percent. Under Angolan law, failure of the top finisher in the presidential election to receive over 50 percent of votes cast requires an election run-off. This has yet to occur because UNITA rejected the results and returned the country to civil war.

The MPLA drew much of its support from the Kimbundu people of Luanda, Bengo, Malanje and Kwanza Norte provinces, while UNITA derived most of its support from its Ovimbundu core areas of Huambo, Bié, Benguela and Cuando Cubango. As the Kimbundu and Ovimbundu ethnic blocks are about the same size, the voting allegiance of the other main ethnic group, the Bakongo, proved critical. While the Bakongo, who are concentrated in the northwest border area, supported Holden Roberto's FNLA in Zaire province (as in the past), outside of that province many Bakongo surprisingly chose the MPLA, instead of the FNLA or UNITA. Moreover, communities worst hit by the war voted for the MPLA and dos Santos. UNITA probably lost votes in the provinces of Cunene, Lunda Sul, Namibe, Moxico and Zaire because people from these areas were under-represented in UNITA's leadership.

Many northern villages balanced a presidential vote for Savimbi against a legislative vote for the MPLA, hedging their bets for the future. However, UNITA did win seventy legislative seats and the vote suggests that if UNITA had accepted the election results, it had made sufficient gains to eventually become a national "peasant party" attracting support beyond its original ethnic base.[4]

THE FAILED DEMOBILIZATION

The weakness of the self-implementing nature of the Bicesse Accords became evident early on when both sides failed to comply with the

---

[4] John Marcum, "Angola: War Again," *Current History*, May 1993; Patrick Smith, "Angola: Free and Fair Elections!," *Review of African Political Economy*, No. 55, November 1992, pp. 101-107.

demobilization plan. The plan called for all of UNITA's 65,000-strong army and the government's 120,000-strong army to be placed first in cantonment areas by August 1, 1991, and then either demobilized or integrated into a single, neutral Angolan Armed Forces (Forças Armadas Angolanas, or FAA) of 50,000 before the September 1992 election. The FAA was to have been comprised equally of government and UNITA personnel.

As the election approached, demobilization was badly behind schedule. As of June 1992, a total of only 20,000 soldiers from both sides had been demobilized. In fact, only 37 percent of government troops and 85 percent of UNITA troops had been put in the forty-eight established cantonment areas, despite the August 1, 1991 deadline.[5] Only 8,800 soldiers had been integrated into the new FAA.[6]

Because the formation of the FAA was a precondition for the September 29-30 elections going ahead, a symbolic creation took place on September 27, with responsibility for the FAA entrusted to the Joint Political-Military Commission (CCPM) overseeing the Bicesse agreements.

Responsibility for the failure to demobilize lies with both the government and UNITA, as well as the U.N. and the international community at large. Both sides were not only uncooperative in the demobilization process, but both apparently were maintaining secret armies in violation of the Bicesse Accords. The government also openly created its new paramilitary police force, the Ninjas.

MPLA Non-Cooperation

Lack of transportation and poor accommodation for demobilizing government forces provoked a crisis in 1992, with soldiers rioting and "spontaneously demobilizing." Although the government maintained a significant fleet of trucks which could transport soldiers, food, and supplies, it was unwilling to contribute to the demobilization process. The government appears to have sold many of its trucks to the private sector.

---

[5] World Bank, "Demobilization and Reintegration of Military Personnel in Africa: The Evidence from Seven Country Case Studies," Discussion Paper, Africa Regional Series, Report No. IDP-130, October 1993, p. 26.

[6] Shawn McCormack, "Change and the Military in Angola: The Impact of the World Order on the Process of Conflict Reduction and Democratization in Angola," paper presented on May 13, 1993 for the Centre for Southern African Studies, University of York (UK) 1992-1993 Research Seminar Series.

U.N. Special Representative Margaret Anstee travelled to Washington in July 1992 to press the U.S. to assist the demobilization effort and the election process. She was able to secure the loan of several U.S. C-130 transport planes which were used to transport troops between July and September. They were, however, often diverted from their scheduled flight plans in order to pick up rioting government soldiers in an attempt to reduce tensions.

Cantonment sites for government troops were mostly disorganized, poorly equipped and understaffed. Lack of discipline, lack of food and low morale were frequently cited by United Nations Angola Verification Mission (UNAVEM) military observers as the major problem in these camps. Moreover, by mid-1992 only two of the sixteen installations designated for the new FAA army had been partially refurbished.

UNITA Delays

In contrast UNITA's army largely remained disciplined and cohesive throughout the interim process, as voluntary demobilization was for the most part not permitted. UNITA continuously delayed mass demobilization, complaining of the lack of guarantees of employment, food and housing for its soldiers. UNITA also refused to use its trucks to assist in demobilization and withheld its trucks from international inspection. In early 1992 UNITA indefinitely postponed the demobilization of many of its forces, citing lack of documentation, funds and civilian clothing as the reason.

There is some evidence that even troops which were publicly demobilized were in fact still held under military discipline, on standby for recall into the uniformed ranks.   UNAVEM officials report that they witnessed UNITA soldiers waiting for further orders from their commanders at the demobilization ceremonies, even after they were technically demobilized. This raises the question whether UNITA ever intended to demobilize its forces fully and whether reports in mid-1992 that UNITA had a secret 20,000-strong army were in fact true. Some of the reports came from defecting UNITA officials N'zau Puna and Toni da Costa Fernandes. Although the Joint Political-Military Commission overseeing the Bicesse Accords investigated these allegations in cooperation with UNAVEM, travelling nation-wide searching for this "army," they were unable at the time to find concrete evidence. However, UNAVEM's intelligence was consistently poor and its capacity to investigate such claims was seriously limited by logistical constraints.

United Nations Ineffectiveness

UNAVEM II was established on May 30, 1991 by Security Council Resolution 696.[7] The U.N.'s main weakness in Angola was its limited mandate. It was restricted to *monitoring and verification* of actions taken by the government and UNITA to implement the Bicesse accords, and of the neutrality of the Angolan police forces.[8]

Many ordinary Angolans mistakenly believed that UNAVEM's role included the power to intervene in disputes. Before and after the elections, international observers saw frustrated Angolans attempting to get UNAVEM to investigate and intervene when political killings and intimidation took place. This led to widespread disillusionment, and even active hostility, to UNAVEM in urban areas. In many such cases UNAVEM under-interpreted its role as it could have mobilized groups of police monitors to investigate complaints. Many Angolans partly blame UNAVEM for the failure of the transition process.

Although interpretations of UNAVEM's mandate differed among UNAVEM officials, it is nevertheless clear that UNAVEM's very presence in itself often acted as an important deterrent against widespread conflict breaking out in the transitional period. During the elections there were occasions when UNAVEM officials found that they had to play a role beyond their electoral observation mandate in the interest of peace, for example by mediating disputes at polling stations or during ballot counting. But, these actions were technically illegal and broke local electoral law.

UNAVEM failed to use effectively the two main weapons within its mandate: public reporting and condemnation of violations and the threat of withdrawal. UNAVEM was virtually silent on human rights abuses, including

---

[7] UNAVEM I was deployed from January 1989 to May 1991, primarily to monitor the withdrawal of Cuban troops.

[8] More particularly, UNAVEM was to monitor and verify:

a) the steps taken by the government and UNITA to ensure the cease-fire, including: termination of hostile actions and propaganda between all parties; confinement of all troops to assembly areas; demobilization and demilitarization of the armies followed by the creation of the new Angolan Armed Forces (FAA); and the collection and disposal of weapons; and,

b) the neutrality of the Angolan police forces, responsible for the maintenance of law and order in the country. Police actions were not to infringe on the political rights of Angolan citizens.

the much publicized murders of Tito Chingunji and Wilson dos Santos.[9] Margaret Anstee, the U.N. Special Representative for Angola, told Human Rights Watch, "The single most important lesson from Angola was that U.N. operations must always have a strong component on human rights."[10]

Threat of withdrawal may not have been a realistic option, as UNAVEM's presence undoubtedly saved lives in areas where it was stationed. Compromise and diplomatic discretion were often UNAVEM's preferred approach. This contributed to both sides increasingly feeling confident enough to violate the peace accords by intimidating suspected opposition sympathizers and not disarming and demobilizing their armed forces properly.

UNAVEM's intelligence was poor. Communication flows between the provinces and its Vila Espa headquarters in Luanda were sporadic; liaison between different departments at Vila Espa itself was often fragmentary due to factionalism among the staff and overly bureaucratic procedures. Many UNAVEM officials were poorly briefed and did not speak Portuguese, let alone a vernacular dialect. This meant many officers relied on locally employed translators. The result was that UNAVEM was generally poorly informed and that when it had valuable intelligence, bureaucratic procedure slowed down decision-making and response.

The U.N.'s attempt to conduct elections in Angola with limited resources is also significant. Margaret Anstee cogently compared her position of having limited resources and mandate with "fly[ing] a 747 with only enough fuel for a DC3."[11]

During the transition, the U.N. maintained only 576 officials, at a cost of $132 million, in Angola, which has a population of about twelve million. By contrast, the United Nations Transitional Assistance Group in Namibia (population 1.5 million) successfully supervised the 1989-90 transition to independence with a budget of $430 million and some 7,150 officials.

---

[9] This downgrading of human rights is not an isolated phenomenon. Human rights often have been given a low priority by U.N. officials who oversee field operations. See, Human Rights Watch, *The Lost Agenda: Human Rights and U.N. Field Operations* (New York: Human Rights Watch, 1993).

[10] Human Rights Watch telephone interview, October 12, 1994.

[11] *Financial Times* (London), May 11, 1992. This was a play on words, with reference to U.N. Security Council Resolution 747 (March 24, 1992) dealing with UNAVEM II's mandate.

Financial and logistical constraints also contributed to the pressure on UNAVEM to push for the holding of the elections on schedule and to plan for a prompt withdrawal. One hundred and eighty-five international observers were flown into Luanda between September 19 and 23, and were budgeted to stay until early October. External events also decisively influenced U.N. decisions. For example, once it became clear that a General Peace Accord was to be signed in Rome on October 4 ending Mozambique's civil war, planning began for shipping UNAVEM equipment and personnel to Mozambique.[12]

THE POST-ELECTION CRISIS: SAVIMBI REJECTS RESULTS

By September 1992, Russia and Portugal had concluded that the election was going to be very close and that UNITA might not win, although U.S. intelligence assessments continued to predict a UNITA victory right up to polling day. It was expected, however, that some sort of compromise power-sharing arrangement would be necessary. Prior to the election both sides said that they were prepared to consider forming a government of national unity.

When the initial returns from the September 29-30 legislative and presidential elections showed the MPLA leading, UNITA refused to accept the results. On October 5, UNITA claimed electoral fraud, pulled its forces from the new joint army (FAA), and threatened to return to civil war.

In response, Western nations and the U.N. pressed behind the scenes for a recount of the Presidential votes and a delay in the public release of the election results scheduled for October 10. Four investigative commissions, plus eighteen provincial teams from the National Electoral Council (CNE), set about investigating UNITA's allegations, supported by international observers. The investigations focused on consistency of voting records, security of ballot boxes, control of surplus electoral kits, and control of supplementary voting stations.

The last count announced by the CNE, before it stopped issuing results, indicated that dos Santos had won the Presidential election with 50.7 percent of the vote. The CNE then reassessed all voting ballots, accepting only those which followed the strictest interpretation of the electoral code. On the recount, the vote for dos Santos fell below the crucial 50 percent mark to 49.57 percent (1,953,355 votes), with Savimbi winning 40.07 percent (1,579,298 votes). By Angolan law, a second round of voting was thus necessary. The MPLA had,

---

[12] See, Alex Vines, "One Hand Tied: Angola and the U.N.," *Catholic Institute for International Relations Briefing Paper*, London, June 1993.

however, won a clear victory in the legislative elections with 129 seats in the 223-seat parliament against 70 for UNITA.

Savimbi agreed to accept UNITA's defeat in the legislative elections in order to participate in the presidential run-off, and announced his intentions on October 16, thereby preempting the CNE's formal announcement of a run-off the following day. On October 17, the U.N. Special Representative officially released the election results and called them "generally free and fair." The Organization of African Unity (OAU), the European Community (EC) and various other international organizations and member states also registered their support for the U.N. verdict.

WAR RETURNS TO ANGOLA

UNITA Offensive and Government Response

In a bid to consolidate control of its strongholds and to take over new areas before a run-off, UNITA launched a military offensive. As early as October 8, UNITA troops occupied Caconda district (Huíla). On October 17-18, UNITA forces attacked in Huambo and by the end of the month fighting had reached Luanda. Intense street battles on October 31 and November 1 in the city center and residential districts left at least 1,200 people dead, many of them civilians.

By November 2 the government's counter-offensive had pushed UNITA troops out of the city into the outer suburbs. The U.N. successfully arranged a ceasefire in Luanda, effective November 3. Fighting for the control of strategic locations continued in other provinces.

Savimbi's nephew and right-hand man, Elias Salupeto Pena, and UNITA Vice-President Jeremias Chitunda were shot dead on November 1 when they were trying to flee Luanda. Savimbi's top military commander, General Arlindo Pena Ben-Ben, escaped injury, but Abel Chivukuvuku, his foreign affairs spokesman, was injured and captured and is now in government custody. The government also holds fifteen other senior UNITA officials, although it has freed several officials, including UNITA's economic spokesperson, Fátima Roque, in a deal.

The government claims that UNITA was attempting a coup d'etat in Luanda, citing the captured diaries of UNITA officials as confirmation. However, an examination by Human Rights Watch of these diaries seems to indicate that UNITA's strategy was brinkmanship designed to force the government into a favorable power-sharing deal. The fact that so many senior

UNITA leaders were in Luanda on October 31 suggests that the fighting caught many in UNITA by surprise.

Regardless of motive or strategy, UNITA's military offensive, which included re-mobilization of its forces, was a clear violation of the Bicesse Accords. The UNITA attack prompted a three-day-long offensive by the Ninjas and pro-MPLA vigilantes (known as "Fitinhas") on UNITA positions in Luanda and in towns across the country. Throughout Angola government supporters razed UNITA offices, killed UNITA officials and purged UNITA from many towns.

Militarily, the government's brief counter-strike was successful not only in decapitating a significant portion of UNITA's political leadership and support structure, but also in destroying UNITA's urban armed militia, known as the Special Security Corp. The government failed, however, to weaken UNITA's regular armed forces (Forças Armadas de Libertação de Angola, or FALA). The MPLA became overconfident that it could militarily defeat UNITA even though it had not yet directly confronted FALA.

Pressure from UNITA's military commanders in the field for a return to full-fledged hostilities against the government grew. Several commanders seem to have started military engagements on their own initiative. For example, UNITA's Provincial Secretary for Kwanza Norte province mobilized FALA forces in Ndalatando once he heard his son had been killed in Luanda by the government.

In Huambo and elsewhere in central Angola, several localized ceasefires were negotiated under UNAVEM auspices in October. Both sides were finding it increasingly difficult to control their regular armed forces and the growing number of armed civilians seeking to settle old grievances. Caxito (Bengo) fell to UNITA on November 4. The following day UNITA captured the town of Porto Quipiri, less than thirty miles from Luanda.

By mid-November the U.N. reported that fifty-seven of Angola's 164 municipalities were under UNITA control and that UNITA maintained an advantage in forty additional municipalities. UNITA also occupied the provincial capitals of Uíge (Uíge), and Ndalatando (Cuanza Norte). In spite of mediation attempts and the Namibe ceasefire agreement, UNITA continued to make territorial gains in the north. UNITA's military successes strengthened the position of hardliners in the MPLA.

Government Counter-Offensive

On December 2, President dos Santos installed a new government. Of the fifty-three members, eleven were affiliated with other parties which had gained seats in the legislative elections. UNITA was offered five posts: the Ministry of Culture and four vice-ministries. Among the other appointments was hardliner General João Baptista de Matos as the new armed forces chief of staff, replacing General António França 'N'dalu, a moderate, who had been negotiating with UNITA in an attempt to try to avoid renewed civil war.

In late December, the government launched its counter-offensive against UNITA, marking a return to full-blown civil war. Fighting spread across the country, with UNITA being pushed back from many locations. The government gained control of Benguela city and Lobito (Benguela province) after fierce fighting. The government's objective was to deal UNITA a final blow on the battlefield and possibly capture Savimbi himself. The government's campaign eventually failed because its forces were over-extended and could not sustain their battlefield gains. By late January 1993, the government was again seeking a negotiated settlement.

UNITA Gains in 1993

On January 28, the U.N. estimated that UNITA controlled 105 out of 164 municipalities. On January 30, UNITA launched its bid to retake Huambo. The city finally fell to the rebels on March 8, at a cost of 15,000 casualties, according to U.N. estimates. UNITA shelled the city relentlessly, despite the fact that the majority of its residents voted for UNITA in the elections. The U.N. Special Representative in Angola described this fighting as the heaviest of seventeen years of civil war.

Throughout 1993 UNITA attempted to gain control of strategic areas outside Luanda. It succeeded in limiting the government's areas of control to mostly coastal areas. The government retained a presence in the towns of Malanje (Malanje province), Menongue (Cuando Cubango) and pockets around Kuito (Bié) and Luena (Moxico).[13] The government still retained control of a sizeable coastal strip from just north of Luanda to the Cunene river border with Namibia. UNITA's strategy was to surround and cut off the cities from the surrounding countryside. Many provincial capitals again became islands of government control in a sea of UNITA domination. Ultimately, it appears UNITA's aim is to control all areas outside Luanda and to bring the economy

---

[13] Kuito (sometimes spelled Cuito) is called Bié by UNITA, as is this province.

to a standstill, creaming off assets—especially diamonds and oil—to fund further conflict with the government and strengthen its hand in negotiations.[14]

Tide Turns Again

But the balance began to change in August 1993, with government forces recapturing large tracts of Benguela, Huíla and Bengo provinces. The government has made further gains in 1994. Between March and July, the area dominated by UNITA was reduced from 60 percent to 40 percent of national territory. Several strategic centers, such as Ndalatando (Cuanza Norte), Cafunfo (Lunda Norte) and several occupied wards of Kuito, were recaptured by the government. The loss of Cafunfo, a key diamond area, was particularly hard on UNITA.

Fighting continues up to the present day, even in the wake of UNITA's September 5 announcement of its decision to accept the proposals on national reconciliation put forth at the Lusaka talks. (See Chapter Seven). The U.N. Security Council, while announcing that with UNITA's acceptance, "the way is now clear for an early conclusion of the negotiations in Lusaka towards a comprehensive [peace] agreement," also stated:

> The Security Council remains deeply concerned by the continuation of the armed conflict in Angola. It reiterates its demand that the parties cease all offensive military actions and reminds them again that all such actions threaten the prospects for a negotiated peace. Attempts to gain short-term military advantage and to procrastinate at the Lusaka peace talks will only prolong the conflict and the continued suffering of the Angolan people and discourage the international community in assisting Angola.[15]

In early October, there was continued progress in the peace talks, particularly on finalizing details regarding control of municipalities. However, fighting continued and the government moved new weaponry and supplies to its

---

[14] For a current assessment of Angola's economic potential, see Tony Hodges, *Angola to 2000: Prospects For Recovery*, Economist Intelligence Unit Research Report, February 1993.

[15] Press statement, SC/5899, U.N. Security Council, 3423rd Meeting (PM), September 9, 1994. The official document is S/PRST/1994/52.

Huambo fronts. Most foreign aid workers were withdrawn from Huambo in September in anticipation of a government assault. UNITA's Political Commission issued a communique on October 4 stating that UNITA was ready to ratify the Lusaka Protocol, on the condition that the government does not attack Huambo. It warned that UNITA would "declare a generalized armed resistance throughout the country, even in Luanda," if Huambo is attacked.

While the government is apparently preparing for a potential assault on Huambo, reports from across the country suggest that UNITA is preparing to return to full-fledged guerrilla bush warfare if it is evicted from the towns. In the cities, such as Huambo, UNITA is cracking down and there has been an increasing number of reports of disappearances and forced recruitment of children.

In Lusaka on October 17, negotiators for the government and UNITA announced agreement on a comprehensive peace treaty, pending approval by leaders in Angola. It appears that both sides are pressing forward on the diplomatic track while preparing militarily for a breakdown in the peace process.

III. MILITARY ORGANIZATION, STRUCTURE, AND OPERATIONS

Reliable information on developments in the organization and structure of government and UNITA forces during the past several years since fighting resumed is sketchy and difficult to obtain. The International Institute for Strategic Studies' authoritative *Military Balance* simply says "current structure unknown" for Angolan forces.[1] But, despite acknowledged gaps in information, some examination of the military organization, structure, and operations is useful to better understand and assess responsibility for violations of laws of war and human rights abuse in Angola. The information that follows is based on interviews conducted during Human Rights Watch's field mission in May and June 1994, unless otherwise noted.

UNITA

Pre-Election Military

In 1991, UNITA's strength was assessed at about 65,000 combat effectives (28,000 regular and 37,000 irregular troops), plus logistical and technical support. Its regular units included twenty or so battalions (*batalhões regulares*) of about 1,000 infantrymen each, plus penetration battalions (*batalhões de penetracao*) and special commandos (*comandos especiais*) for specialized tasks. The irregular units were grouped into semi-regular battalions (600 infantrymen each) and guerrilla forces. These included compact guerrilla companies (150 per group) and dispersed guerrilla companies (15 to 50 per group). All UNITA military forces were supported by paramilitary militia, the "Peoples' Sentinels" (Sentinelas do Povo).[2]

UNITA's artillery units were divided into three specialized types: field artillery (*artilharia terrestre*), air defense artillery (*artilharia anti-aérea*) and anti-tank artillery (*artilharia anti-tanque*). UNITA also had a combat

---

[1] International Institute for Strategic Studies, *The Military Balance, 1993-1994* (London: Brassey's, October 1993), p. 199.

[2] John Turner, "Angolan Vs. Angolan: Battle of Mavinga," *Museum Ordnance*, Vol.2, No.3, May 1992; IISS, *The Military Balance, 1992-1993*, p. 191.

demolitions/special forces unit, called the Action Brigade for Explosive Techniques (*Brigada de Acção Técnica de Explosivos*, or BATE), and a military intelligence service *(Serviços de Inteligência Militar*, or SIMI). There were also military police and communications, logistics, personnel and training commands.[3]

Artillery and anti-tank support were highly flexible. While heavy artillery was used for sieges and conventional engagements, lighter systems were used to support blocking forces that were threatened with mechanized attack. UNITA mounted recoilless rifles on four-wheel drive vehicles, especially Toyota Land Cruisers, and employed them in highly mobile tank-killer battalions. UNITA called these units "hunter" (*Caçador*) battalions.

Current Operations
UNITA's armed forces have apparently retained much of their previous basic organizational structure since the elections and resumption of fighting, but UNITA has devised new strategies and opened new operational fronts. UNITA's military operations are now divided into four operational fronts.

 • The Northern Region is split into the following sectors: (1) Uíge and Zaire provinces under the Command of General Dembo; (2) Cuanza Norte and Bengo under General Numa; and (3) Malanje siege under the command of General Chimoco.

 • The North Eastern Region (Lunda Norte and Sul and Moxico) is under the command of General Nyemba.

 • The Eastern Region (Moxico).

 • The Central Region (Benguela, Bié, Cuanza Sul, Huambo and Huíla) is technically overseen by Savimbi. However, General Consagrado is directing the military sieges of Kuito and Cunje (Bié province), and there are other commanding generals in Ukuma, Bolombo and near Waku Kungo.

UNITA's Head of Operations, Brigadier General António Manuel Urbano, nicknamed "Chasanha," explained to Human Rights Watch in May 1994 that UNITA did not maintain a Southern Region because of the negligible threat to it there from the government forces. However, operations by UNITA in June and July suggest that UNITA has now opened a front in the south.

The Front Commands appear to have autonomy with respect to day-to-day operations. But, Savimbi is clearly the commander-in-chief with overall military responsibility. Human Rights Watch was told by several UNITA

---

[3] John Turner, "Angolan Vs. Angolan," May 1992.

military officials that Savimbi travels to sensitive fronts to make his own assessments.

Other key UNITA military leaders include: General Dembo, the UNITA Vice-President, who has responsibility for northern operations and the far north in particular; General Ben-Ben, the General Command's Chief of Staff; General Sapalalu Bok, Savimbi's Chief of Staff; and, Deputy Secretary of Defense General Chilingutila, who is UNITA's senior military tactician.

According to UNITA, any sensitive military intelligence, such as the capture of "foreign mercenaries" or reports of human rights brutalities, would go to Savimbi's Chief of Staff Bok before reaching the Military General Staff. The Military General Staff is itself divided into different departments such as operations, intelligence, health, and logistics. Each regional zone's staff is similarly organized, with the Front General being the ultimate authority for the zone's security issues and discipline issues.

GOVERNMENT FORCES

Prior to the May 1991 Bicesse Accords, the government's armed forces, known as FAPLA *(Forças Armadas para a Libertação de Angola)*, numbered an estimated 127,500, including 120,000 ground forces. Between May 1991 and the elections in September 1992, the Angolan government largely neglected its regular armed forces, which were supposed to be demobilizing and integrating into the new, unified Angolan Armed Forces (FAA), and failed to maintain its existing military equipment. Instead, the government focused on equipping and training the Rapid Intervention Police (Ninjas). After the elections, the government initially relied heavily on the Ninjas and on the armed urban populace to fulfill combat roles. But, as fighting expanded, the government invested heavily in the regular army. By 1994, the army had been retrained and rearmed under the banner of the FAA, while the power and influence of the Ninjas waned.

The government's military strategy is primarily one of "selected offensives" designed to reduce UNITA's capability to operate on more than one front at a time. A logistical blockade of the central plateau is combined with intensive air bombing attacks designed to reduce supply deliveries to UNITA. There has also been a campaign to destroy UNITA's weapons stockpiles, logistical depots, and principal military bases in central Angola.

Reflecting this strategy, General João de Matos, Armed Forces Chief of Staff, said on February 23, 1994, that he believed that UNITA would only commit to a peace accord if it was at a military disadvantage. He said, "If there is military equilibrium, which is what we have at the moment, there will not be a lasting agreement.... It is necessary to have a military imbalance to reach an agreement." But, significantly, he also added that, in the end, "There is no military solution for Angola."[4]

In 1994, the army remains hampered by logistical shortcomings as well as a shortage of troops, making it difficult for it to prevent reinfiltration of many areas it has taken. The current number of troops is estimated at 60,000, and some analysts believe that at least 100,000 men are needed to sustain fighting and consolidate captured areas. The government's attempt to draft 30,000 new recruits by July 1993 was not successful, and the Ministry of Defense decreed on April 21, 1994 the mobilization of youths born in 1974. The general service requirement for all Angolan males over twenty years of age is for three years. They then remain in first-line reserve status to the age of thirty-four, second-line reserve status until age thirty-nine, and third-line reserve status until age forty-five.

Ground Forces

FAA units are currently engaged on eight operational fronts. While the Angolan government has not released detailed information on all its operational fronts, most can be identified from battle reports. Each operational front has a Command Post (*posto de comando* or PC), which controls a task-organized force. The general term for task-organized forces is no longer "*agrupamento*," as it was for the old FAPLA army, but rather "*Grupo*" (Group).

Each Grupo is comprised of motorized (*Motorizada*) or light (*Ligeira*) infantry regiments, which are in turn comprised of battalions. It is believed that the FAA has 22 regular regiments, plus two Special Forces regiments. For large or permanent operations, each Grupo PC can place elements of its force under one or more Forward Command Posts (*posto de comando avançado* or PCA).

One example of a PCA is Lukala II (named from a bridge over the river) in Cuanza Norte, which was overrun by UNITA on June 18, 1994. Among the items UNITA claimed to have captured were twelve tanks and twelve 82mm mortars, indicating the PCA had armor and artillery units attached to it. Lukala II was a PCA for over eight months, and had directed three of the past four assaults on Ndalatando.

---

[4] *Reuters*, February 24, 1994.

Northern Front
Luanda

Under the FAPLA, Luanda was designated a Special Defense Zone (*Zona de Defesa Especial* or ZDE). This was revived in late 1993. Units dedicated to the defense of the capital include armored and mechanized units, which are likely similar to FAPLA's Special Defense Brigade, and are probably under direct control of the Angolan Armed Forces General Staff (EMGFAA). The city is also defended by the Presidential Guard, which also has armored and mechanized units. Under FAPLA, the Presidential Guard was brigade-sized, but now it is a full regiment. Armored and mechanized units from the ZDE and the Presidential Guard were used in the unsuccessful attack against Ndalatando at the end of April 1993.

At least five regular FAA regiments, each about 2,000-strong, exist in the Luanda area, controlled by a PC located between Luanda and Caxito. One, a motorized infantry regiment, is apparently located at the PC. The remaining four are light infantry regiments, two based in the Caxito area and two in the Dondo-Cambambe area.

In addition, the Katangese Brigade, also known as the "Tigres," is based in the Luanda area, with its headquarters at Viana. It is comprised mainly of former FNLA soldiers. The strength of the 1st (and presumably only) Katangese Brigade is estimated to be 1,400, divided into at least three battalions. Like the southern Angolans who make up the majority of Presidential Guard, the Katangan soldiers are a trusted group. UNITA claims that Cuban and Katangese mercenaries are being used in the current offensive in Cuanza Norte province. They are said to be operating jointly with the FAA and Riot Police to re-occupy Cuanza Norte. It appears that many of the troops known as "Katangese" are Zairian refugees or former soldiers drawn to this French-speaking unit; the original Katangan Gendarmes, who fought in the late 1970s, are well past their retirement age.

Soyo and Cabinda

Under the old FAPLA, two brigades of infantry plus several territorial battalions were based in Cabinda. It is likely that at least one relocated to Soyo. Two infantry regiments of over 1,000 men each were defeated by UNITA in Soyo on June 24, 1994, when it recaptured the town. The troops were probably withdrawn to Cabinda.

Northeastern Front—Central Malanje Province

The Malanje area is the base of three regiments: one at Quessua-Malanje guarding the city, one on the Cacuso-Malanje axis, and one on the Cangandala-Mussende axis. FAA forces from the 2nd FAA Motorized Infantry Regiment are responsible for defending the city. This regiment is probably that which the media calls the 43rd Regiment.

Central Front
Cuanza Sul Province

Fighting in this region has been taking place on the Quibala-Waku Kungo axis and on the Sumbe-Gabela axis. Despite fierce UNITA resistance, FAA forces are advancing in the Waku Kungo area, while at the same time attempting to cover their flanks with operations in Quilenda and elsewhere. The FAA is also launching attacks from Sumbe to Gabela and Conde in an attempt to disrupt UNITA forces. Air assault forces are active between Catofe and Quibala.

Benguela

The FAA column advancing on Huambo in October 1994 numbers about 10,000, organized into at least five regiments of troops. There are four axes: Ganda, Bocoio (Benguela), Waku-Kungo (Cuanza Sul), and Huíla. Both light and motorized infantry are operating on this front. A light infantry group, supported by a battalion of motorized infantry and two air squadrons, has been attempting to move past Quilengues to secure the area as a base for attacks into Huambo province. As part of this operation aircraft from Lubango Air Base are bombing surrounding areas in an attempt to "soften up" targets before ground action.

During late 1993 at least two separate task-organized FAA groups were operating out of the Benguela-Lobito area, the 8th Technical Group on the Bocoio-Balombo axis, the other to the south on the Cubal-Ganda axis. It is possible that FAA also has at least five regiments in the Lobito-Benguela-Catumbela area, one of which is motorized.

Southern Front—Northern Namibe/Lubango

In April 1993 two brigades in this area were operating against UNITA along the railway. That month UNITA alleged that a joint FAA-Namibian army operation was in progress along the border involving four brigades of joint FAA and Riot Police. The affected area was between border markers 2c and 46. Human Rights Watch has been unable to confirm these reports. When asked by Human Rights Watch in late 1993 about UNITA's allegations, the Namibian

Foreign Minister said that his diplomats had held talks with UNITA in Europe in an attempt to stabilize the situation. UNITA subsequently stopped alleging Namibian involvement in the conflict.

Lubango has its own task-organized forces. At least four and perhaps as many as six FAA regiments are stationed in the western half of the Southern Front (or perhaps four regiments and two task-organized groups). Elsewhere Regimental headquarters also exist at Menongue, Kuito and Luena. The only provinces which are unlikely to have regimental headquarters are those under more or less firm UNITA control: Uíge, Zaire and Huambo.

Special Forces

The FAA Special Forces (*Forças Especiais*) are, like the old FAPLA Special Forces, elite units which have had commando training and specialist instruction in unconventional warfare. Like the Presidential Guard, they are the last line of defense (and trust) for the government. Most of the Special Forces are deployed around Luanda. The Special Forces headquarters is probably co-located with the FAA's general HQ in the city. There is apparently one Special Forces Regiment made up of several Groups. In early 1994, the Second Special Forces Group concluded its training course at Cabo Ledo and was sent to the field. In addition to standard infantry weapons, the special forces use helicopters backed by PC-7 counterinsurgency/reconnaissance aircraft.

"FAA Special Airborne" units have been mentioned several times in the press. Airborne units recaptured Cafunfo, Lussamba, and Cuando in a series of attacks. They are inserted by helicopters, backed by PC-7 counterinsurgency/reconnaissance planes, and equipped with light infantry weapons, such as 82mm and 60mm mortars and PKM machine guns. Their mission includes disruption of UNITA rear areas and the laying of antitank and antipersonnel mines.

The Air Force

The Air Force has an important operational role in the current conflict. At one point, the Angolan Air Force was a large and powerful force, with about 200 combat aircraft and forty armed helicopters. But, the Air Force had deteriorated greatly, with over seventy aircraft non-operational because of a lack of spare parts and poor maintenance. Only two of some two dozen Mi-25 attack helicopters were operational in November 1992.

Massive investment and new imports since have developed the Air Force's operational capability, especially with new purchases of Mi-24 and Mi-25 helicopter gunships. The helicopters, as well as MiG-23 and Sukhoi-22 fighter-bombers, have been widely used in the war. UNITA alleges that Swiss PC-7 and TC-7 aircraft have also been used in offensive action against it. Human Rights Watch openly watched Su-22s and MiGs depart from Luanda's Quatro de Fevereiro International Airport on bombing missions. The aircraft would typically take off with bombs mounted on the external weapon pylons, head north, and return some sixty to seventy minutes later, without their bomb loads. The government has also launched air raids from Catumbela, Lubango and Saurimo.

FOREIGN SECURITY PERSONNEL AND EXECUTIVE OUTCOMES

A South African "security consultant" firm, Executive Outcomes (EO), has apparently provided armed personnel to assist both UNITA and government forces. An oil industry source told Human Rights Watch that in late 1992 and in early 1993, EO was providing assistance to UNITA on contract. Then, in February 1993, the government hired 100 expatriate armed personnel through EO to protect privately-owned oil installations in Soyo. Thus, in the first quarter of 1993, EO employees found themselves assisting operations against each other. In April 1993 EO reportedly ended its work with UNITA. EO has expanded its activities in Angola during 1994, and its contract with the government is reportedly worth some $40 million per year.[5]

UNITA now alleges that personnel from Executive Outcomes are mercenaries.[6] The government and EO call them "security consultants."

---

[5] *Le Monde* (Paris), July 8, 1994. EO employees were initially offered 60-day contracts with payments of up to $5,000 per month. See also, *The Weekly Mail and Guardian* (Johannesburg), September 16-22, 1994, which claims that a new 12-month contract was signed at the beginning of September 1994.

[6] "Mercenary" is defined in Article 47 of Protocol I to the Geneva Conventions of 1949:
Article 47 — Mercenaries
        1. A mercenary shall not have the right to be a combatant or a prisoner of war.
        2. A mercenary is any person who:
        (a) is specially recruited locally or abroad in order to fight in an armed conflict;
        (b) does, in fact, take a direct part in the hostilities;
        (c) is motivated to take part in the hostilities essentially by the desire for private gain and, in fact, is promised, by or on behalf of a Party to the conflict, material

Salaries for EO employees in Angola reportedly range between R10,000 and R40,000 (about \$3,300-\$13,300) per month.[7] The government denies that it has ever hired mercenaries. The Deputy Foreign Minister Jorge Chicote told Human Rights Watch at Cambridge University on March 21, 1994, "We cannot guarantee the security of private enterprise in Angola. We therefore encourage them to make their own arrangements." EO's general manager maintains that its activities are simply above-board training and advice, and that when employees have "had to fight," it was in self-defense or incidental to training and advice on the battlefield.[8]

EO was founded in 1989, reportedly to train South African special forces. It is made up of former members of South African units such as Koevoet, 32 Battalion, and the Civil Cooperation Bureau (CCB).[9] EO's Director is Eeben Barlow. Nico Palm is its Financial Manager and Lafras Luitingh, a former CCB member, is responsible for "Operations." Karl Deats, a spokesman for EO, described his organization in an interview on SABC-TV on June 3, 1994, saying, "Our function over here comprises a couple of things, first of all, in an advisory capacity. Secondly, in a socio-economic assistance role, and then the main function that we had over here is to conduct training."

EO now has some 400-500 men in Angola. Since mid-1993 EO has trained 4,000 to 5,000 government troops and about thirty pilots. Training takes place at three camps, located in Lunda Sul, Cabo Ledo and Dondo, and reportedly includes basic fighting techniques, weapons maintenance, signals,

---

compensation substantially in excess of that promised or paid to combatants of similar ranks and functions in the armed forces of that Party;

(d) is neither a national of a Party to the conflict nor a resident of territory controlled by a Party to the conflict;

(e) is not a member of the armed forces of a Party to the conflict; and

(f) has not been sent by a State which is not a Party to the conflict on official duty as a member of its armed forces.

[7] *The Weekly Mail and Guardian* (Johannesburg), September 16-22, 1994.

[8] *The Weekly Mail and Guardian* (Johannesburg), September 16-22, 1994.

[9] Koevoet, or Crowbar, was the former police anti-insurgency unit in Namibia. The 32 Battalion consisted of members of the defeated National Front for Liberation of Angola (FNLA) who were integrated into the South African military after 1976, and fought in Angola against the MPLA. It was disbanded in April 1993. The CCB was a South African intelligence hit squad.

engineering, and specialized skills such as sabotage. In addition, EO is said to be training the FAA "Reconnaissance Regiment," which was used in an offensive against Ndalatando in March 1993, and FAA "Special Tactical Intervention Units." A former Portuguese commando, Marcelino de Mata, is reported to be training these units at Dondo. EO is also helping to set up an intelligence structure in Luanda. EO routinely flies three 737 aircraft from Lanseria airfield (near Johannesburg) into Angola.

EO also maintains two "Special Units" of its own, which since February 1994 have been active in front-line operations against UNITA. One was deployed in Uíge province, the other in Lunda Norte province in August 1994. Human Rights Watch has been told that three ex-SADF helicopter pilots regularly transport both EO employees and Angolan soldiers, including in combat situations.[10]

According to a detailed story in the Johannesburg *Weekly Mail and Guardian*, EO's "most glaring success" was the recapture of Cafunfo, the center of the diamond trade in Lunda Norte province, in July 1994. The operation was carried out by the FAA's 16th Brigade, which had been completely regrouped and retrained by EO, and EO assisted with the planning of the mission. According to the story, an EO employee acknowledged that "about twenty Executive Outcome 'advisers' had been spread through the column, from platoon to command level, and air support had been given by Executive Outcomes-trained pilots. Two company employees were wounded."[11]

Sources have told Human Rights Watch that EO has assisted the Angolan government in weapons procurement. This may be the "socio-economic assistance" referred to by Mr. Deats.

In April 1994 the Johannesburg newspaper *Die Beeld* claimed that former EO employees had been threatened with death if they talked about their operations in Angola.[12] The paper alleged that in January 1994 men employed by EO were informed that they might have to participate in offensive action against UNITA. A group of about twenty who refused returned immediately to South Africa. A second group returned some weeks later after they also refused to fight against UNITA.

---

[10] Interview in Johannesburg, September 1994.

[11] *The Weekly Mail and Guardian* (Johannesburg), September 16-22, 1994.

[12] *Die Beeld* (Johannesburg), April 7, 1994.

Human Rights Watch has obtained a copy of an eight-point "Agreement" which EO required its employees to sign. It states, "The member accepts that the duties requested in terms of this agreement may [be] extremely dangerous in nature and could even lead to death." It also states that the member "undertakes not to divulge any information relating to this contract or his duties to any person or body. Should this undertaking be breached, the member will forfeit his salary and will pay an amount of R 100,000.00 [about $30,000] as liquidated damages to the company."

Three EO employees were killed in combat with UNITA in early March 1994 and three more were wounded and flown to Windhoek, Namibia on March 7 for medical treatment. The Windhoek-based National Society for Human Rights (NSHR) voiced its concern in July 1994 about Namibian nationals working as mercenaries for EO.[13] It revealed that three Namibians, Geraldo "Peugeot" Alfredo of Windhoek, Albertus Steyn Marais of Otavi, and Renier van der Merwe of Windhoek, "had died, disappeared or had been captured during offensive military skirmishes against UNITA in Angola." The NSHR is also verifying allegations that another Namibian national, Dolf van Tonder, and at least five others have disappeared during military operations in Angola.

UNITA claims to have killed over 125 "foreign mercenaries" in the past fifteen months. EO's Eeben Barlow admits that fifteen of his employees have died in Angola from malaria, training accidents and UNITA attacks since mid-1993. In September 1994, another EO representative said that fourteen employees had died in Angola in the past year.[14]

UNITA currently holds two EO employees prisoner. One has been identified by UNITA as D.C. O'Connell, a South African. He and a colleague were captured on July 15, 1994 when their PC-7 plane was shot down by UNITA shortly before government forces recaptured the strategic diamond town of Cafunfo. Since January 1993 UNITA has publicly been threatening to execute any captured mercenaries. Following a July appeal for clemency by South African Deputy President Thabo Mbeki, UNITA announced it would not execute them, but urged the South African government to prohibit EO from sending personnel to Angola. In August the South African Department of Foreign Affairs was negotiating for their release, although one was feared dead.

---

[13] National Society for Human Rights, letter to Hon. Minister Theo-Ben Gurirab about "Namibians Serving as Mercenaries in the Angolan Armed Conflict," July 5, 1994.

[14] *The Weekly Mail and Guardian* (Johannesburg), September 16-22, 1994.

In late July 1994, the South African Department of Justice announced it had started investigating the activities of EO. The South African Foreign Affairs Department has strongly criticized EO, characterizing its operatives as "mercenaries," and saying that it wants them out of Angola because they undermine South Africa's new image as an impartial regional power.[15] The South African Department of Foreign Affairs issued a statement on September 21, 1994 saying, "The government is in principle opposed to its citizens being involved in internal conflicts in Southern Africa, and the activities of Executive Outcomes reduce the ability of the government to play a credible and constructive role in supporting the peace process in Angola." The statement further said that the government opposed EO's involvement in Angola "even for the purposes claimed" by the company, and that, "their activities will therefore continue to be the subject of close scrutiny by government agencies."[16]

Mercenary activities are outlawed in Namibia and South Africa under sections 43 and 123 of the Defense Amendment Act (Act No.20 of 1990) and Defense Act (Act No.44 of 1957). Both the Namibian and South African governments are under obligation to take decisive steps against any persons, organizations or even states that engage in mercenary activities.

The United Nations frowns on the use of mercenaries. The U.N. Special Rapporteur on the use of mercenaries in his 1993/4 report concluded that "with regard to the aggravation of this armed conflict, the presence of foreign mercenaries who have participated in training operations and in combat has been a key factor in the duration and nature of the conflict."[17] The evidence on the ground indicates that although mercenaries are not the deciding factor in the war, they do make a difference in the military operations in which they participate.

---

[15] Ibid.

[16] SAPA News Agency, Johannesburg, in English, 1839 gmt, September 21, 1994.

[17] "Report on the question of the use of mercenaries as a means of violating human rights and impeding the exercise of the right of peoples to self-determination," submitted by Mr. Enrique Bernales Ballesteros, Special Rapporteur, pursuant to Commission resolution 1993/5. E/CN.4/1994/23, January 12, 1994. See also, *U.N. International Convention on the Recruitment, Use, Financing and Training Of Mercenaries*, 1990.

IV. ARMS PROCUREMENT

The renewed conflict, and accompanying human rights abuses and violations of laws of war, are being fueled by new flows of arms into the country. The May 1991 Bicesse Accords prohibited both the government and UNITA from acquiring new weaponry (the "Triple Zero" clause), and the U.N. Security Council imposed an international arms embargo on UNITA in September 1993. Yet, both sides have been procuring arms and foreign expertise for some time. In January 1993, United Nations Security Council Resolution 804 noted that "there are also disturbing unconfirmed reports that...new supplies of arms may be entering Angola."

The government is now using its oil revenue to buy weapons at a record level, while UNITA is using its access to diamond-producing areas to fund its purchases of weaponry.

THE GOVERNMENT

According to the U.S. Arms Control and Disarmament Agency (ACDA), Angola imported $4.6 billion in arms in the five years before the Bicesse Accords (1987-1991). About 90 percent ($4.1 billion) came from the former Soviet Union. Other Warsaw Pact nations provided $80 million in arms, West European nations $80 million, and Latin American nations $370 million.[1]

ACDA's figures show the government's foreign arms purchases declining drastically during this period, from $1.7 billion in 1987 and $1.6 billion in 1988, $750 million in 1989, $490 million in 1990, and $30 million in 1991.[2]

---

[1] U.S. Arms Control and Disarmament Agency, *World Military Expenditures and Arms Transfers, 1991-1992* (Washington, D.C.: U.S. Government Printing Office, March 1994), p. 131. According to the annual editions of the Stockholm International Peace Research Institute's *SIPRI Yearbook, World Armaments and Disarmament* (New York: Oxford University Press), during this period Angola's non-Warsaw Pact acquisitions included armed helicopters from France, PC-7 aircraft from Switzerland, transport aircraft and fast attack boats from Spain, and maritime patrol aircraft from Brazil.

[2] ACDA, *World Military Expenditures and Arms Transfers, 1991-1992*, p. 94.

Prior to the Bicesse Accords, the government's armed forces numbered about 127,500, including 120,000 ground forces. Main equipment included about 500 tanks, 150 BMP-1 armored personnel carriers (APCs), 250 other APCs including BRDM-2 reconnaissance vehicles, 500 heavy artillery pieces, at least 100 multiple rocket launchers (MRLs), SA-7 and SA-14 surface-to-air missiles, plus a large assortment of other Warsaw Pact weapon systems. The standard tank was the T-54/T-55, although elite units had some T-62s. By 1989, the BTR-60PB APC was being phased out of front-line units in favor of the BMP-1. Artillery consisted mainly of D-30 122mm howitzers, M-46 130mm howitzers, M-1942 (ZIS-3) 76mm howitzers, and BM-21 MRLs.[3]

With Angola returning to full-fledged civil war in January 1993, the Angolan government re-embarked upon an international weapons shopping spree. On April 23, 1993, the government unilaterally declared that the Triple Zero clause in the Bicesse Accords was obsolete and that it would no longer abide by the arms embargo. Luanda called on "all countries with which the Angolan government has diplomatic relations of cooperation to help it to equip its forces with material and logistical means." During the summer of 1993, all of the members of the Observing Troika (U.S., Russia, and Portugal), as well as other nations such as the U.K., announced a lifting of their national bans on military supply to the Angolan government.

Military analysts estimate that the government purchased some $2.5 billion in weapons in 1993. Purchases between January and July 1994 are estimated at an additional $1 billion. Comprehensive information on arms flows to the Angolan government in the last two years is impossible to obtain, but Human Rights Watch has been able to gather sufficient details to illustrate the types of equipment the government is purchasing, the suppliers, and the methods of acquisition. It is evident that the government is continuing to purchase a full range of weaponry, from small arms and ammunition to tanks and aircraft. The government is buying weapons from numerous sources, including governments in Europe, Africa, Asia, and Latin America, although much of the weaponry is purchased from private international arms dealers. Most of the arms deals are cloaked in secrecy and subterfuge; many involve false documentation. Many involve multiple governmental and private actors. The Nora Heeren shipment is a good case in point.

---

[3] See, Fred Bridgeland, *Jonas Savimbi: A Key to Africa* (Edinburgh: Mainstream Press, 1986), pp. 413, 443; and, IISS, *Military Balance 1992-93*, p. 191.

The Nora Heeren

The Nora Heeren, a freighter registered in Oldenburg, Germany, was chartered by an Antiguan-registered company. The freighter sailed originally from IJmuiden in the Netherlands on December 13, 1993, and docked at Vysotsk, Russia on December 21. There it took on a cargo of weapons produced in the Russian Federation and the Czech Republic. It left Vysotsk on December 29, bound for Angola. The Nora Heeren would not have attracted international interest if it had not been impounded on January 11, 1994 in the British port of Plymouth for not having the correct cargo papers. The captain had declared that the ship was carrying "agricultural equipment," when in fact it was carrying weapons for the Angolan government. Still, once its papers were put in order, the ship was allowed to sail in mid-January.

Human Rights Watch has compiled a partial list of the ship's cargo, which one private source has told Human Rights Watch is worth an estimated $100 million. The shipment included:

- 30 T-55 and T-62 main battle tanks
- 40 BMP-1 armored fighting vehicles
- 20 M-46 130mm artillery pieces
- 20 ZSU-23-4 23mm anti-aircraft guns
- 1,000 100mm shells for T-55 main guns
- 1,000 122mm artillery shells for D-30 guns
- four million rounds of 7.62mm. ammunition for AK assault rifles
- instruction manuals and spare parts for the arms and equipment being shipped.

The cargo was unloaded in Luanda in February 1994. Some of the arms and equipment was moved to the airport under tight security and airlifted to an unknown destination by an Antonov-22.

In a similar incident, a Belize-registered ship was detained briefly by Turkish customs authorities on May 27, 1994. The Bulgarian captain admitted that his cargo was Bulgarian weaponry and that he was sailing to Angola. Human Rights Watch has been informed that this ship was one of five due to set sail for Lobito from Bulgaria. It should be noted that although the ship's captain declared his cargo as Bulgarian, it is possible that some or all of the weaponry originated from elsewhere.

Since the Nora Heeren incident the Angolan government has switched the bulk of its weapons shipments to Benguela and Lobito from where the supplies are transported to the military fronts or put into store.

Africa's Number One Arms Buyer

Weapons procurement by the government has reached record levels, surpassing even the extraordinary years of the mid-1980s when the Soviet Union was flooding the Angolan government with weaponry, often without requiring payment, as part of a key superpower proxy war. The government of Angola has unquestionably been the largest arms purchaser in Sub-Saharan Africa during the past two years. In December 1992, with war against UNITA opening up on all fronts, the government decided it needed to rebuild and retrain its armed forces. During the transition period, the government had allowed its army's weaponry to deteriorate, while building up, with Spanish help, the paramilitary Rapid Intervention Police (Ninjas). Thus, throughout 1993, the government's arms purchases were primarily aimed at replacing obsolete and poorly maintained equipment.

In January 1993, responsibility for arms purchasing was shifted from the Armed Forces General Staff, headed by General João de Matos, to the Defense Ministry in an attempt to regulate procurement more closely. This has not occurred. Many officers in the General Staff logistics and procurement unit simply transferred to the Defense Ministry.[4] Procurement has continued to be chaotic and poorly coordinated, with senior government and military officials sometimes carrying conflicting or duplicate lists on their shopping missions.

The record level of arms imports does not necessarily mean that all the weapons are destined for the battlefield. It appears that since late 1993 the government has been buying weapons that are not immediately required for the current conflict. Much of the new weaponry has yet to appear on the battlefronts. The enormous quantities of war material being purchased with such evident urgency by military and government officials may be at least partially explained by potential profits involved. Human Rights Watch has received reports that a recent first-time purchase of advanced T-72 tanks was clinched as much for the commission payments to those settling the deal as for the strategic need. A freelance arms dealer told Human Rights Watch in June 1994 that Angolan clients of some of his business associates looked for 15-30 percent kick-backs in any contract.[5]

While individuals may be making large profits on arms deals, the Angolan government appears to be undermining its economic future through

---

[4] "Old Marxist slams Angola corruption," *Africa Analysis*, February 18, 1994.

[5] Chief of Staff Gen. João de Matos when interviewed about corruption in the army denied any knowledge of it. *Jornal de Noticias* (Lisbon), February 11, 1994.

massive arms imports. The *Financial Times* has reported that the government produces more than 500,000 barrels a day of oil, worth about $2.75 billion per year, but that more than 60 percent has gone directly to the defense budget.[6] An international weapons dealer told Human Rights Watch in June 1994 that the government was issuing tenders for weapons on short-term loans, mortgaged against potential future oil production with short-term letters of credit. A United Nations source in Luanda told Human Rights Watch that the next seven years of oil production have been mortgaged in this manner. Estimates based on Angola's current oil reserves indicate that production may last only fifteen years.

Arms Suppliers

It is clear that many nations, as well as private companies, are involved in selling and shipping arms to the government of Angola. One press account in September 1994 noted, "Arms shipments from Spain, Israel, Brazil and the former Soviet Union are being unloaded openly at Luanda's airport."[7]

During its May-June 1994 field mission to Angola, Human Rights Watch openly observed large amounts of military equipment, including artillery pieces, being unloaded from Antonov and Ilushin planes with markings from the Russia, Ukraine, Bulgaria, and Uzbekistan. It was not possible to determine the precise types of arms, or the manufacturer, with certainty, but the national origin of the transport aircraft involved clearly implicates those governments in the arms trade business in Angola.

Russia

Russia appears to have inherited from the former Soviet Union the distinction of being the largest arms supplier to Angola. Vice-Minister for Defense Pedro Sebastião visited Moscow in August 1993, one of many such visits by Angolan officials in 1993.[8] In its submission to the United Nations Register of Conventional Arms, Russia reported deliveries in 1993 to the Angolan government of twenty tanks, thirty-five armored combat vehicles, and fourteen large´caliber artillery systems. (See below for more on the Register). This listing appears to be very incomplete, given the widespread observations of massive Angolan purchases of Soviet-style weaponry in 1993.

---

[6] *Financial Times* (U.S. edition), September 2, 1994.

[7] Ibid.

[8] *O Independente* (Lisbon), August 6, 1993.

The Nora Heeren shipment detailed above may be typical of recent Russian-Angolan deals. It is known that one single recent deal was valued at $180 million. Russia is providing the full range of conventional weaponry to Angola, including some advanced weapons not seen in Angola before, such as the T-72 tank. A correspondent for the Lisbon *O Público* reported in August 1994 that he saw Russian Mi-17 helicopters, tanks and artillery pieces being openly off-loaded from ships in Luanda's port.[9] New purchases of Mi-24 and Mi-25 helicopter gunships have made a significant difference to Angola in its battlefield operations.

Reportedly, a contract signed between the Angolan military procurement agency, SIMPORTEX, and a Franco-Russian consortium in late July 1994 calls for four shipments of weaponry, including Mi-17 helicopters and armored personnel carriers.[10] A Portuguese weekly has reported Russian involvement in a $100 million arms deal with Angola that also involves Portugal and Brunei. (See below under "Portugal").

The weaponry that UNITA claims to have captured recently continues to be overwhelmingly of Soviet/Russian manufacture. In 1994, in broadcasts from its Voice of the Resistance of the Black Cockerel (Vorgan) radio station, UNITA claimed to have captured or observed in government possession the following Soviet systems: M-46 130mm field guns; D-30 122mm artillery guns; BM-21 122mm multiple rocket launchers; 76mm cannons; 14.5mm cannons; 60mm and 82mm mortars; RPG-7 40mm rocket propelled grenade launchers; AGS-17 30mm grenade launchers; AKM 7.62mm assault rifles; and, PM Makarov 9mm pistols. UNITA also claims to have captured 23mm cannons, 120mm mortars, and South African-made R-5 5.56mm rifles.[11]

When a Portuguese radio journalist interviewed Aldmiro da Conceição, a spokesman for the Angolan presidency, on July 24, 1994 about the morality of Russia, a Troika member, providing weapons, the reply was:

> [Conceição]: The Angolan government has been resorting to the international weapons market to acquire the necessary means to defend itself in this war against UNITA. This is legal and legitimate, especially after the U.N. approved

---

[9] *O Público* (Lisbon), August 17, 1994.

[10] *Expresso* (Lisbon), July 30, 1994.

[11] FALA General Staff Communique, August 26, 1994.

the election results and lifted the arms embargo against the Angolan government.

[journalist]: Do you not feel that this is a little awkward, when Russia is a member of the Troika of observers of the peace process? Could this not discredit Russia's impartiality in the process?

[Conceição]: No, Russia no longer has the privileged position it had in the past, when the Soviet Union existed. At the moment Russia has a totally different position and we have resorted to the international weapons market where Russian arms are available...[12]

Brazil

Two ships containing Brazilian weapons shipments docked in Lobito in January 1993, suggesting that Brazil sold weapons to the government of Angola in late 1992, in violation of the Bicesse Accords Triple Zero embargo.

The Brazilian press have reported that the Angolan government obtained 6,000 X-40 and X-60 rockets in July 1993, manufactured by the Brazilian firm Avibras at a cost of $160 million (or about $26,000 per rocket). As of September 1993, only one shipment had been made. Luanda may also have purchased twenty launching trucks, also produced by Avibras. At $200,000 each, these trucks contain a computerized firing control panel. The rocket sales were approved by Brazil's intelligence service (Itamaraty), Army Ministry, Armed Forces chief of staff, and Strategic Affairs Secretariat. The X-40 is supposed to be capable of hitting a target forty kilometers away with only a two-meter margin of error to each side.[13]

In February 1994, the FAA Chief of Staff General João de Matos paid an official visit to Brazil. In an interview he described the visit as "exploring the possibilities of military cooperation," and said that the visit was a success.[14] The London-based *Jane's Intelligence Review* reported that the purpose of the visit was "to negotiate further supplies of arms and ammunition, continuing

---

[12] RDP Antena-1 Radio, Lisbon, in Portuguese, 1900 gmt, July 24, 1994.

[13] *Veja* (São Paulo), September 15, 1993, and *Jornal de O Dia* (Lisbon), September 13, 1993.

[14] *Jornal de Notícias* (Lisbon), February 11, 1994.

procurement of over $100 million since mid-1993."[15] In May 1994 the government agreed to a contract with Embraer for six "Tucano" reconnaissance aircraft. President dos Santos visited Brazil to sign the contracts.

When Human Rights Watch visited Huambo, fragments of several air-to-ground rockets could be seen on the grounds of Huambo's Central Hospital. UNITA also displayed a whole rocket that had failed to detonate.[16] Human Rights Watch believes this rocket is a Brazilian-manufactured SBAT-70 M2 rocket, produced by Avibras-Indústria Aeroespacial SA.

North Korea

North Korea also appears to be emerging as a major supplier of arms to the Angolan government. In reply to a parliamentary question, the British Minister for Overseas Development, Baroness Chalker, wrote on April 26, 1994: "The Angolan army is believed to have purchased substantial quantities of arms from North Korea." The Portuguese press has reported that the Angolan government purchased some $95 million dollars worth of weapons from North Korea in 1993, including SA-2 missiles and BMP-1 and BMP-2 armored fighting vehicles, and received training for Angolan fighter pilots as well.[17]

Human Rights Watch has been told that Angola has recently provided North Korea with a substantial "shopping list" of North Korean weaponry. Human Rights Watch understands from several sources that Uzbek planes have been commissioned by the North Korean government to transport weapons purchased from Pyongyang. In May 1994, Human Rights Watch openly observed weapons being unloaded from Uzbek aircraft at Luanda's Quatro de Fevereiro International Airport.

Portugal

UNITA has regularly claimed that the government of Portugal has been active in weapons deals with the Angolan government. The government denies that it has provided arms, although it acknowledges that it has provided, and continues to provide, a wide variety of military training. This training has

---

[15] "MPLA Government Presses for a Military Solution in Angola," *Jane's Intelligence Review POINTER*, No. 6, April 1994, p. 1.

[16] On the head of the rocket was written: Cabeça de Guerra/ Lote: 93/ Validade: 06-96. On the body: Motor Foguete: 70mm/ Lote: 06-93 No: 125947/ Validade: 06-96.

[17] *O Independente* (Lisbon), January 14, 1994.

reportedly included infantry reconnaissance and ambush training by Portuguese paratroopers, training of naval/marine cadres, navigation and strategic planning for air force personnel, and training for the Angolan special police by the Special Operations Groups of the Portuguese Public Security Police.[18]

In July 1994, the Portuguese weekly *O Independente* reported a complicated arms deal involving Portugal, Brunei, Russia, and Angola.[19] This investigative report was based on a leaked secret official memorandum. It alleged that, through Investimentos e Participações Empresariais (IPE), a Portuguese State-owned company, Sociedade Portuguesa de Empreendimentos (SPE), acted as the intermediary in setting up a commercial deal between a financial adviser of the Sultan of Brunei, José António Saraiva, the Russian government, and an Angolan government delegation led by Vice-Minister for Commerce Paulino Baptista, assisted by the Vice-Minister of the Armed Forces General Staff, General José Maria. The deal, initially agreed to in February 1993, was a financial package for industrial supplies to Luanda and possible investment in a new oil refinery, but also included a protocol for military assistance.

According to the report, on March 16, 1993 an Angolan government delegation led by Gen. José Maria returned to Geneva to finalize the details and to hold meetings with members of a firm called Intora Ltd (49 percent owned by the Russian government) over developing Russian/Angolan co-operation. The delegation flew on to Moscow from Geneva, accompanied by João Serra of SPE. A further military assistance protocol was signed in Moscow between the Angolan delegation and Intora on April 1, 1993. Such assistance was in violation of the Bicesse Accords Triple Zero clause.

The agreement reportedly included arms sales worth $100 million for T-62 tanks, light antitank missiles, BMP-3 armored personnel carriers, and 20mm cannons for helicopters with 40,000 rounds of ammunition. According to a memo sent on September 8, 1993 from SPE to the President of IPE, Amaro de Matos, much of this equipment was second-hand and in poor condition, for which the Angolan government had made a down payment of $10 million. The down payment was made through the Banco Nacional de Angola (BNA) to Blic Bank - Republic National Bank. It was then transferred to the National Bank of Luxembourg and into the account of the Rothbury Finance Corporation. The balance of payment was to be divided between a $50 million credit facility

---

[18] *O Diabo* (Lisbon), October 7, 1993.

[19] *O Independente* (Lisbon), July 8, 1994.

arranged by António Saraiva and $40 million pledged by a note of credit issued from the Banco Nacional de Angola.[20]

The Portuguese government has issued several denials of involvement.

Spain

Spain's Rural Anti-terrorist Group of the Guardia Civil trained the Angolan government's Rapid Deployment Police (Ninjas) in 1991 and 1992. In 1991 Spain exported through Defex, the state weapons firm, 640 million pesetas (about $6 million) worth of arms; in 1992 this increased to 2,634 million pesetas (about $26 million). In 1993 these exports were estimated to be worth 2,353 million pesetas (about $20 million). According to Spanish security officials this material was for the police and included pistols, flak jackets and anti-riot equipment. In 1992 Spain also sold vehicles to the military and police, including Santana Landrovers, at a value of 708 million pesetas (about $7 million).

With Spanish government clearance, the private Spanish firm Ekinsa also sold Angola $40 million in security equipment, including $8 million in arms, between 1991 and 1993. According to Ekinsa's director, Cesar de la Prida, his company's relationship with Angola started in 1986 and peaked in 1991 with the signing of a protocol between the Angolan government and his firm which now acts as "official parallel representative" of Angola's Ministry of the Interior. Ekinsa was involved in the training in 1992 of the Ninjas by the Guardia Civil. The Spanish government has classified as secret any additional details.

In May 1994 a scandal erupted over the activities of the former Director General of the Guardia Civil, Luis Roldan, in trying to procure weapons for the Angolan government in late 1992 and early 1993. In late 1992 Roldan had been approached by an Angolan government delegation, led by the then Angolan Minister for Foreign Affairs, Van Dunem "Loy," and Francisco Paesa, a Spanish national. Paesa, who is at present an adviser to the Angolan ambassador to France, has on several occasions undertaken sensitive missions on behalf of President dos Santos. He has also acted as dos Santos' special envoy to Israel.

Roldan admits that sometime in late 1992 he received a sixty-page request for arms from General Carlos Rubio of the Spanish Civil Guard, after Rubio had been received in Luanda by dos Santos and Paesa. The first phase of the request, worth $200 million, included armored personnel carriers, mortars, heavy machine guns, antitank guns, antipersonnel mines and radios. Roldan

---

[20] *O Independente* (Lisbon), July 22, 1994.

denies that he subsequently attempted to push for the export of $60 million of arms, including anti-aircraft guns, combat vehicles and artillery of various calibers. In early 1993 private and state-owned firms, encouraged by Roldan, began to put together a shipment. Only when one of the companies involved attempted to get export permits from the Spanish Ministry of Foreign Affairs did the deal fall through. After a prolonged debate the Ministry ruled that no permits could be issued because this breached the then operational Triple Zero clause ban on weapons sales to Angola.

In August 1993, a month after the ban was lifted, the government issued a license to the company Defensa y Exportacion to export weapons to Angola up to the value of $60 million. As of May 1994 deliveries had not been made. UNITA has claimed that Uzi-type submachine guns manufactured in Spain have been captured by their forces.[21]

Other Nations

• UNITA alleges that Argentina has supplied weapons to the government. Human Rights Watch has been unable to verify this.

• Bulgaria has reported to the United Nations that in 1993 it provided Angola with twenty-four T-62 tanks and twenty-nine BMP-1 armored fighting vehicles, and that it also delivered 21 BMP-1s manufactured by Belarus.

In mid-September 1994, it was reported that a shipment of 250 tons of missiles worth over $7 million belonging to the Angolan Ministry of Defense was stranded in Cyprus. The missiles reportedly had been loaded in Bulgaria aboard a Cypriot-registered ship, but were off-loaded in Cyprus due to a dispute over freight charges, and were put into storage until a new carrier could be found.[22]

• The Czech Republic has acknowledged importing seven BVP-2 armored combat vehicles from Hungary and then re-exporting them to the government of Angola in 1993.

• As noted above, it has been reported that the Angolan government signed a contract with a Franco-Russian consortium in late July 1994 which calls for four shipments of weaponry, including helicopters and armored personnel carriers.[23] The Zairian opposition has alleged that France is supplying UNITA

---

[21] *El Pais* (Madrid), May 15, 1994; *Expresso* (Lisbon), June 18, 1994.

[22] "Missiles Bound for Angola Stranded in Cyprus," *Reuters*, September 14, 1994.

[23] *Expresso* (Lisbon), July 30, 1994.

with weapons redirected from shipments previously destined for Rwanda. No credible evidence has been provided.

  • Angola established diplomatic relations with Israel in 1992. Since then there has been widespread speculation about Israeli arms sales to the government, but little hard evidence.[24] In December 1992 a ten member Angolan delegation, headed by António dos Santos França, visited Israel. In early 1993, Galil rifles appeared in combat zones. Human Rights Watch observed Galils in the hands of some Rapid Intervention Police and soldiers deployed in Luanda.

  • German-manufactured G3 rifles reportedly have been purchased from Nigeria.[25]

  • There is widespread speculation that since late 1993 South Africa has been exporting weapons to the Angolan government, in a dramatic reversal of nearly twenty years of direct support with arms and manpower for UNITA. Some of the small arms that government soldiers use that look like Israeli models could be South African-manufactured copies. South African R4 and R5 rifles, for example, are copies of Israeli Galils. On the other hand, Armscor appears to have been shipping weapons in late 1992 and in 1993 to southern Zaire, and some believe that this material was destined for UNITA.

  • In July 1994 UNITA, which had received an estimated $250 million in U.S. military assistance from 1986 until 1991, began to allege that U.S.-manufactured weapons were appearing in the hands of government forces. On July 3, 1994 UNITA claimed to have captured U.S.-made antitank weapons from government parachute drops in Kuito.[26]

  • For more than six months, Ukrainian border guards have impounded a Russian cargo ship, the Modul, citing "irregularities." It is loaded with fifty-nine tons of ammunition, mostly 7.62mm, that is officially registered as

---

[24] "Israel is now arming Angola," *Israeli Foreign Affairs*, Vol IX, No.4, May 11, 1993.

[25] See, for example, *O Independente* (Lisbon), August 6, 1993.

[26] Voice of the Resistance of the Black Cockeral, in Portuguese, 0600 gmt, July 3, 1994. UNITA claims the antitank weapons were inscribed with the numbers M1.1.02004.91A43, SEOPR1811K161.91 and the numbers 36 and 133.

belonging to the export branch of Ukraine's military. The cargo is destined to be shipped to the Angolan government.[27]

• Zimbabwe Defense Industries appears to have sold ammunition and some bombs to the Angolan government, and shipped them via Ndola in Zambia.[28]

UNITA

Before Bicesse, UNITA had three main sources of weapons: those captured from the Angolan government, and those supplied by South Africa and the United States. U.S. covert aid to UNITA totalled about $250 million between 1986 and 1991, making it the second largest U.S. covert program, exceeded only by aid to the Afghan mujahidin.

While UNITA has fielded some armored and mechanized units with T-54/55 tanks and armored personnel carriers, most UNITA forces have been light infantry backed up by artillery, air defense and antitank units. UNITA has used captured 122mm D-30 artillery and 122mm BM-21 multiple rocket launcher systems widely, as well as 75mm and 76mm field guns, and 82mm and 120mm mortars.

U.S.-made 106mm recoilless rifles mounted on four-wheel-drive vehicles have been particularly popular with UNITA. Shoulder-fired light antitank weapons (LAWs), as well as RPG-7 rocket launchers have provided additional firepower. UNITA has also utilized captured air defense artillery and shoulder-fired surface-to-air missiles (SAMs)—including captured SA-7s and U.S.-supplied Stingers. The Stingers given to UNITA reportedly were returned to the U.S. in late 1990 after the Bush administration came under intense domestic pressure and requested them back. Human Rights Watch has been told that the Stingers were exchanged for less sensitive lethal equipment.

The Angolan government claims to have captured from UNITA in 1994: U.S.-made antitank missiles; 75mm, 80mm, 106mm, and 120mm artillery pieces; 60mm, 81mm, and 82mm mortars; U.S.-made M-60 grenade launchers; RPG-7 rocket launchers; PKM machine guns; AKM rifles; and, German G3 rifles.

---

[27] *RFE/RL Research Institute Military Notes*, No.151, August 10, 1994.

[28] Human Rights Watch interview with Zimbabwean official, Harare, May 1994.

Sanction-Busting

In addition to the May 1991 Bicesse Accords which forbade the purchase of arms by both sides in Angola, on September 15, 1993, the U.N. Security Council adopted Resolution 864 prohibiting the sale and supply of any military or petroleum products to UNITA.[29] However, UNITA continues to break U.N. sanctions on a substantial scale, most often through Zaire. Supplies on a far smaller scale have also reached UNITA from South Africa, although these shipments declined in 1994 as the South African elections approached. In many cases, private dealers may be flying in shipments to UNITA-held airstrips by filing false flight plans with the South African, Zairian, and other governments.[30]

It is very difficult to establish in conclusive detail recent arms acquisition by UNITA. It is clear that UNITA continues to capture significant amounts of weaponry from the government. Much of the weaponry seen in the hands of UNITA by Human Rights Watch appeared well maintained, but not new. In particular, Human Rights Watch noted large numbers of AKMs and RPG-7s in the hands of UNITA combatants which were most likely captured from the government.

UNITA has also been active on the international arms market in 1993 and 1994, using cash obtained from the sale of diamonds to buy weapons and ammunition from private sources. Among other things, UNITA appears to be buying new D-30 120mm artillery and replenishing its stocks of surface-to-air

---

[29] U.N. Security Council Resolution 864, Article 19 states that the Security Council: "Decides, with a view to prohibiting all sale or supply to UNITA of arms and related materiel and military assistance, as well as petroleum and petroleum products, that all States shall prevent the sale or supply, by their nationals or from their flag vessels or aircraft, of arms and related materiel of all types, including weapons and ammunition, military vehicles and equipment and spare parts for the aforementioned, as well as of petroleum and petroleum products, whether or not originating in their territory, to the territory of Angola other than through named points of entry on a list to be supplied to the Government of Angola to the Secretary-General, who shall promptly notify the member states of the United Nations;"

[30] Human Rights Watch has, however, investigated official public statements by the Zimbabwean government in late 1993 that it had concrete evidence of such flights. Our inquiries in Zimbabwe established that the strategic radar installations at Thornhill were not operational when the government claimed it had monitored the information. This suggests that these claims were made from solidarity with the Angolan government rather than fact.

missiles, both of which have been used by UNITA to force suspension of humanitarian aid flights to besieged government-held towns.

UNITA has lost the unconditional support of its two major governmental arms suppliers—the United States and South Africa—but UNITA continues to receive support from private sources in South Africa, and has found a number of other governments willing to provide arms, or to facilitate UNITA's arms purchases through private sources, most notably Zaire. Other nations apparently involved, directly or indirectly, in arms supply and sanction-busting in Angola include Congo, Namibia, Russia, China, and perhaps many others. Military assistance to UNITA violates mandatory United Nations sanctions.

Arming UNITA

Zaire: Diamonds, Arms, Bases, Troops

Since the United States and South Africa ceased their major military assistance programs, Zaire has become the most important source of support for UNITA. UNITA uses Zaire as a transit area and conduit for diamond sales and weapons transfers, maintains a number of small rear bases in Zaire, and receives operational support from Zairian troops.

The U.N. Security Council announced on July 15, 1994, that it had evidence of possible sanction violations through Zaire and Congo.[31] Later that month, an Italian ship sailing from Antwerp and destined for the Zairian port of Matadi was detained by the Angolan authorities. German boats and trucks were confiscated because the authorities suspected they were destined for UNITA. According to the ship's register the equipment was destined for a religious congregation in Zaire.[32] According to some sources, UNITA in 1994 shipped 120mm D-30 artillery through Kinshasa's Ndjili international airport. It has also been alleged that Chinese arms are being provided to UNITA through Zaire (see below).

Human Rights Watch has been told that many flights destined for UNITA zones were using Ndjili International Airport in Kinshasa, Zaire. The cargo on many of these flights appears to be fuel and lubricants, which are items on the sanctions list. Human Rights Watch interviewed one person who flew out of UNITA zones in April 1994 on one of these flights. She described the aircraft

---

[31] U.N. Security Council, July 15, 1994, (S/1994/825).

[32] *Expresso* (Lisbon), July 30, 1994.

as an Electra L188 carrying forty to sixty empty oil drums. The oil drums smelt of petroleum and had recently been emptied because they were damp from spillage. The pilots boasted of doing this flight four times a week to airstrips like Cafunfo or Andulo. This particular firm called itself the Trans-Service Airlift.

In a presentation on May 31, 1994, the Angolan government submitted to the U.N. Security Council a list of companies whose flight activities Angolan Ambassador to the U.N. Afonso Mbinda claimed were "proof involving the current Zairian regime in support for UNITA, in flagrant violation of the arms and fuel embargo imposed by the Security Council." Ambassador Mbinda alleged these companies used Kinshasa's Ndjili International Airport and the airstrips G652D and UG652D.[33] The companies named were:

• Trans-Service Airlift (TSA).   Aircraft: Electra L188 (9Q-CCV); L188 (9Q-CRM); Viscount V744 (9Q-CVF).   Crew: Cowez; Terken; Ramaekern; Tys.

• Guila Air.   Aircraft: Nordatlas N2501 (9Q-CKO); (9Q-CNE); (9Q-CCD); Viscount V744 (9Q-CGA).   Crew: Koch; Marsal.

• Trans-Air Cargo (TAC).   Aircraft: Britania-31 BR31 (9Q-CJH).

• Utair.

• PAE.   Aircraft: Ilyushin Il-76 (RA 76510).

• Blue Air Line (BAL).   Aircraft: Electra L188 (9Q-CDG); (9Q-CDI). Crew: Vanderset.

Ambassador Mbinda claimed that this "direct involvement by Zaire in the destabilization of Angola is an act of aggression against my country, according to the definition of aggression given by the United Nations in 1974."

Moreover, Human Rights Watch has obtained credible evidence that UNITA retains minor rear bases in Zaire near Boma and Banana from which to operate in Cabinda. These are small with thirty or so UNITA soldiers present at any one time. According to local people, the bases have been there for over five years. The bases are so well established that they have regular standing orders for fish and other supplies.

Elements of the Zairian military have provided support, if not direct combat assistance, for UNITA military operations. An expatriate oil worker told Human Rights Watch that after UNITA captured Soyo on January 19, 1993, he saw Zairian units cross from Soyo at night into Zaire in a "flotilla of boats, tugs and dug-out canoes laden with booty. Fridges, air conditioners, computers, even window frames. You name it. If it could be moved they took it. I am told these

---

[33] See also, Sharon Beaulaurier, "Profiteers Fuel war in Angola," *Covert Action*, Summer 1993.

were members of Mobutu's Presidential Guard, but it was dark and they looked like mean soldiers to me. I didn't hang about and ask them." Huge amounts of equipment and material from Soyo ended up in Kinshasa's main markets a week later.

The Angolan government has frequently alleged that Zairian units are fighting for UNITA, but Human Rights Watch has been unable to obtain concrete evidence that President Mobutu has ordered Zairian troops to engage in direct combat in support of UNITA. In Soyo, for example, Zairian soldiers did not appear to be involved in offensive action against the government. They may have been brought into Angola to take their "cut" in booty as payment for previous favors their commanders had shown to UNITA, such as giving them rear base facilities. UNITA may also have recruited individual Zairians into its ranks on a paid basis as mercenaries.

In addition, UNITA purchases oil products in the Zairian ports of Matadi and Boma, shipping them across the river to its zones to be transported to the military fronts. In a bizarre interlinking of the adversaries' economies, state-owned coasters sail from Luanda to deliver their oil cargo in Matadi, which is then bought by UNITA in violation of the U.N. sanctions.

In an unmistakable sign of the changing situation, on May 26, 1994, Pete Smith, marketing director for Armscor, South Africa's state arms procurement agency with responsibility for certifying arms exports, stated at a Pretoria news conference, "We suspect Zaire is a conduit for weapons to UNITA leader Mr. Savimbi and we will not provide weapons to Zaire until we are satisfied where they are going."[34]

South Africa
It is widely suspected that elements within the South African Defense Forces continued to covertly supply UNITA for several years following the Bicesse Accords.[35] Armscor also appears to have been shipping weapons in late 1992 and in 1993 to southern Zaire, and some believe that this material was destined for UNITA.

In December 1992 the governments of Angola, Zimbabwe, Namibia and Botswana made accusations that South African aircraft were violating their

---

[34] *O Pensador* (Washington DC), Vol. 2, June 1994.

[35] See, for example, Mats Berdal, "The Resumption of Civil War in Angola," *Jane's Intelligence Review*, June 1993, pp. 284-5. Berdal specifically accuses the SADF's Directorate of Military Intelligence.

airspace in support of UNITA. The South African government denied these charges but admitted that private operators could be doing this. On January 23, 1993 the Angolan government issued a list of South African companies it believed to be involved in illegally ferrying weapons to UNITA: Avalon Tours, Barbian Aircraft Company, Southern Air Transport, Professional Air Services, Westair, and Wonder Air. The Angolan government also named individuals it said were involved in the operations as pilots and engineers.

A list of aircraft involved in activities in support of UNITA was also provided:

Four four-engine Douglas DC-6 cargo planes (Registrations V5-NNC and N44DG, two unknown);

Three Cessna 310s (Registrations V5-JJL, V5-ZPK, V5-FUR);

Two Cessna 402s (Registrations ZS-RAN and V5-NCE);

Cessna 210P (Registration ZS-KIW);

Cessna 210 (Registration V5-JCT);

Cessna CE 208 (Registration V5-NCE)

Beechcraft Kingair 200 (Registration Ni-5587);

Learjet LR 24B;

Learjet 24 (Registration V5-KJY)

Subsequently, in March 1993, President dos Santos publicly accused Wonder Air, a South African chartering company, of flying illegal UNITA resupply flights. The registered owners of Wonder Air are Gert de Klerk (a close associate of then-Foreign Minister Pik Botha) and former Defense Minister Magnus Malan. On March 23, 1993, the Angolan authorities also detained a DC-3 (Registration ZS-KCV) belonging to the South African company Professional Aviations under charges of transporting individuals and supplies into UNITA territory twenty-seven times between October 27 and December 15, 1992.

In early October 1994, *The Weekly Mail and Guardian* (Johannesburg) reported that Angolan armed forces intelligence chief "General Itha" had provided the newspaper with a list of companies, individuals and aircraft he claimed were involved in "covert support" of UNITA. Itha alleged that military equipment, food and medicine were being flown from South Africa mostly to Zaire, and then transported to UNITA bases in Angola. Intha's list included Zairian, Namibian, and South African-registered aircraft.[36]

---

[36] *The Weekly Mail and Guardian*, September 30-October 6, 1994.

In 1992 and 1993 the Angolan government claimed that South African mercenaries were fighting for UNITA.[37] As discussed above, Executive Outcomes was apparently working with UNITA in the first quarter of 1993. But by mid-1993 EO had reportedly severed all its links with UNITA, after securing a substantial security contract with the Angolan government. EO's Director Eeben Barlow claims that members of South Africa's Military Intelligence are still in 1994 supplying UNITA forces and a waging an undercover campaign against his company because he supports the Angolan government.[38]

In early October 1994, there was widespread press coverage of a fraudulent shipment of Armscor weapons that supposedly were bound for Lebanon aboard a Danish ship (Aktis Pioneer), but instead ended up in Yemen, and may originally have been intended for UNITA. After being turned away from the Yemeni port of Al Hudaydah, the ship returned to Port Elizabeth, South Africa. Armscor claimed that it had been duped by a Middle East arms dealer, Eli Wazan. South African Defense Minister Joe Modise ordered an investigation of the matter, reportedly "because he and his cabinet colleagues are said to be deeply concerned about reports that Armscor has been trying to sell 25,000 AK-47 and G-3 rifles and some 13 million rounds of ammunition to the Angolan rebel movement UNITA as well as to Middle Eastern countries."[39] On October 13, Justice Minister Dullah Omar announced the appointment of a

---

[37] "Report on the question of the use of mercenaries as a means of violating human rights and impeding the exercise of the right of peoples to self-determination," submitted by Mr Enrique Bernales Ballesteros, Special Rapporteur, pursuant to Commission resolution 1993/5' document E/CN.4/1994/23, page 18, para. 41, is incorrect. Three mercenaries named in the report, Geoffrey Landsberg, Hermanus Ferreira and Nico Bosman were injured in Soyo defending oil installations against UNITA attack, not fighting for UNITA in Huambo according to Angolan government sources in May 1994. This contradicts earlier government statements to the media about this incident.

[38] *The Weekly Mail & Guardian* (Johannesburg), July 29-August 4, 1994.

[39] *The Star* (Johannesburg), October 1-2, 1994. According to another report, Armscor has said that the consignment consisted of 8,596 AKs, 15,665 G3s, and 14 million rounds of ammunition. *The Weekly Mail and Guardian*, October 7-13, 1994. Yet another report indicated 9,200 AK-47s, 15,600 G3s, and 14 million rounds of ammunition. *Washington Times*, October 11, 1994.

commmission of inquiry to look into this shipment, as well as other Armscor transactions since January 1991.[40]

According to EO's Eeben Barlow, UNITA ordered the guns from Armscor, without the government's permission, in May 1994, but was subsequently unable to pay for the weaponry, which was being offered at the discounted price of R2.3 million (about $700,000). Barlow claims that he was approached to buy the shipment, and that it eventually was sent to Yemen.[41] The media has also cited intelligence sources, arms brokers, and arms trade researchers on the UNITA connection.[42]

Namibia

It was reported in October 1994 that the government of Namibia closed the border with Angola to prevent illegal arms deliveries to UNITA. On October 10, military police questioned four men arrested on suspicion of smuggling military equipment to UNITA. They were stopped at a roadblock at Chito, about six miles from the Angolan border, although a truck accompanying the men managed to escape the roadblock. According to Namibia's Army Chief of Staff Major General Ndaxu Namoloh, Namibian soldiers had also seen at least three small aircraft flying to and from the approximate position of Savimbi's headquarters of Jamba during the previous week.[43] Another report indicated that the border was closed in early October after an attack in Namibia, presumably by Angolan military, left three people dead and a woman raped.[44]

Rundu, Namibia continues to be used as a UNITA supply point. The Angolan government claims that the crews file fictitious flight plans, stating a return itinerary from South Africa to Luanda via Rundu, while in fact they fly into UNITA-controlled zones, using Rundu as a refuelling stop. On March 10,

---

[40] SAPA news agency, Johannesburg, in English, 1355 gmt, October 13, 1994.

[41] Ibid.

[42] Ibid. See also, *The Sunday Times* (Johannesburg), October 2, 1994; *The Weekly Mail and Guardian*, September 30-October 6, 1994, and October 7-13, 1994; and, *The Daily Telegraph* (London), October 3, 1994.

[43] *Reuters*, October 10, 1994; SABC Radio South Africa, Johannesburg, in English, 1500 gmt, October 10, 1994.

[44] World Food Program Situation Report, Angola as of October 5, 1994.

1994 Namibian authorities grounded an Antonov-26 and its Russian crew, chartered by the South African-based firm Ecomex, on charges of supplying UNITA. Medical and radio equipment were confiscated by the investigating police. An Antonov-32 with a South African crew was impounded on March 19.[45]

Human Rights Watch saw evidence of the ongoing trade links in Huambo with northern Namibia, particularly Rundu. Although much of the trade is not prohibited by U.N. sanctions (notably beer, medicine and stationery), petroleum products have been regularly purchased by UNITA from Rundu dealers since October 1992. Although these petroleum purchases have declined since October 1993, they continue. An Angolan refugee who had recently fled from Jamba told Human Rights Watch in May 1994: "We still get our fuel from Namibia. Now that flights have declined we have to make the land trip. Our biggest problem is cash to pay for what we need." Credit facilities with border businessmen apparently dried up in 1993.

Russia

It has been reported that UNITA has purchased weapons from Russia, and that Russian aircraft have also been used to transport other nations' weapons to UNITA, most notably South Africa. The Moscow-based firm Ecotrends (with a New York office called Global Trends), which has a contract with Safair in Johannesburg, has been involved in ferrying weapons to the Angolan government and possibly also UNITA. Four AN-124 Antonovs, with the services of sixty Russian aircraft pilots, have been leased to South Africa for freight route traffic.

South African journalists Gavin Evans and Eddie Koch reported in February 1993 that ten Russian Antonovs, each with a capacity of seventeen tons, had used South Africa's former Bophuthatswana homeland since May 1992 to ferry weapons to Zaire and other African countries, with some of the weapons destined for UNITA.[46] They witnessed an Antonov 12 at Mmabato which had just returned from a trip to Kinshasa, Zaire. Regular night flights were being made from Mmabato to southwestern Zaire.

A South African civil aviation official claimed to journalists that the Antonovs were being chartered directly by Armscor and some other African

---

[45] Rádio Nacional de Angola, Luanda, in Portuguese, 1900 gmt, March 20, 1994.

[46] *The Weekly Mail*, February 26-March 4, 1993.

countries to fly weapons produced by Armscor out of the "homeland" to other African countries:

> This is useful to Armscor because it means their arms are being transported by Russian aircraft, which are far less conspicuous. Their crews are always based in Bophuthatswana, they don't need South African work permits or South African pilot's licenses, and we have no jurisdiction over them.[47]

Bophuthatswana's Civil Aviation Director, Dermott Maclaughlin, claimed that these Russian planes were being used for humanitarian flights under U.N. auspices and that they were owned by Africa Aeroflot. Africa Aeroflot and the U.N. have denied they were operating humanitarian flights from Mmabato; it appears that the names of both organizations have been used as a smoke-screen for illegitimate flights out of South Africa. At least one other Russian-registered Antonov was grounded in 1993 on suspicion of unauthorized flights to southern Zaire. This aircraft, registration number CCCP 48059 and leased by the South African firm Del Industries, was detained at Durban. It had recently used Mmabato airport.

Because the route used by these flights passed over South Africa's Bophuthatswana "homeland," Botswana and northern Namibia, the South African government initially claimed ignorance of these operations. But by 1994, with the collapse of the Bophuthatswana homeland regime and the build-up to the South African elections, there has been a significant decline in flights of this kind from Mmabato, according to airport staff interviewed by Human Rights Watch.

United Kingdom

In 1993 a network of small companies linked to the Johannesburg Bias group, a conglomerate run by industrialist Christopher Seabrooke, was alleged by the *Guardian* newspaper of London to have been acting as contractors buying what were described as relief supplies and airlifting them into rebel territory. The Johannesburg Bias group has defense industry links.[48] An invoice from December 1992 showed that the contractor for delivery of a shipment of relief

---

[47] Ibid.

[48] *The Guardian* (London), March 13, 1993.

aid into rebel areas was Merchant International Trading Inc. Company records show that it shares offices, directors and shareholders with six other British-registered companies. The principal one among these is Merchant Trade Finance, part of the investment arm of Bias. One of Merchant Trade Finance's big investments in South Africa was the engineering firm Helcial. When Helcial collapsed in 1990, its managing director, Robert Taylor, revealed that it had "extensive" contracts with Armscor.

Other Nations

● An Executive Outcomes employee, Karl Deats, claimed in June 1994 that Chinese weapons and ammunition have been brought into UNITA territory from Zaire.[49] In April 1993, the government captured light and medium artillery of Chinese manufacture from UNITA in northern Angola. However, these arms may not have been acquired directly, or recently, from China. In May 1993, the Chinese Embassy in Luanda denied it supplied arms to UNITA.[50]

● Like the government, UNITA has reportedly been active in weapons transactions with the Ukraine and Bulgaria.

● The Zairian opposition has alleged that France is supplying UNITA with weapons redirected from shipments previously destined for Rwanda. No concrete evidence has been provided.

Diamonds for Arms Deals

Diamonds sales enable UNITA to pay for weapons, as well as oil and lubricants, obtained in violation of international sanctions. The De Beers diamond cartel and other international dealers are buying gems mined in rebel-held territory in violation of Angolan law. Intermediaries have made payments of hundreds of thousands of dollars to UNITA officials for diamonds smuggled across Zaire's southern border. In January 1993, UNITA officials were reportedly paid $400,000 in cash by dealers in the Zairian town of Tshikapa, about seventy miles from the Angolan frontier. Lebanese dealers working as licensed traders in the town claim that one-third of the diamonds they handle comes from Angola, almost all from UNITA zones. According to a report in the *Financial Times*, about $250 million worth of diamonds came out of Angola in

---

[49] *Jane's Defence Weekly*, June 18, 1994, p. 19.

[50] *Reuters*, May 5, 1993.

1993, mostly from the Cafunfo area, which was under UNITA control until captured by the government at the end of July 1994.[51]

De Beers closed its office in Tshikapa in January 1993 because of "insecurity," but it continues to liaise with the local dealers. De Beers has admitted spending $500 million to buy legally and illegally mined diamonds originating in Angola in 1992 in "open market transactions."[52]

A similar trade is carried out along the Zambian border where Zambian diamond entrepreneurs send teams of traders, often Senegalese, Malian or Zairian, into UNITA areas to make diamond deals in violation of Angolan law. One good diamond can procure a truck load of sugar or mealie meal on the flourishing barter market. When visiting the border in May 1994, Human Rights Watch was told that isolated UNITA units trade in this manner, with the dealers arranging the portering caravans or lorries to carry supplies across the border. The trade routes now go as far as Huambo, Kazombi and Kavungu. However, weapons do not appear to be traded along Zambian cross-border trade routes in any significant quantity.

When asked about diamonds, senior UNITA official Jacka Jamba told Human Rights Watch in Huambo:

> Sanctions don't work because of diamonds. We have many.
> We have also invested in training some of our cadres on what
> is a good gem. Those Lebanese can't so often cheat us. We
> know what we are selling.

A London-based diamond trader told Human Rights Watch that when he dealt with a UNITA official in 1992 before the elections, he was surprised by the level of technical knowledge the latter had shown.

It appears that there has been a significant decline in UNITA's diamond output since 1992, as the diamond-producing areas have become theaters of conflict and UNITA has redeployed people from the diamond fields into military

---

[51] *Financial Times* (U.S. edition), September 2, 1994. Another source reports that UNITA exchanged an estimated $200 million worth of uncut stones for small arms, support weapons and ammunition in 1993. *Jane's Defence Weekly*, September 10, 1994, p. 22.

[52] *The Guardian* (London), March 4, 1993. De Beers claims that it is buying the diamonds in order to stabilize the market, since thousands of quality Angolan gems reaching the open market could force international prices to crash.

operations. But the income received from diamond sales in all likelihood continues to exceed the cash value of aid formerly provided by the United States, which totalled an estimated $250 million from 1986 to 1991.

TRANSPARENCY IN ARMS TRANSFERS

Human Rights Watch believes that states should be willing to provide details about their weapons transfers and other military assistance to other countries. As a rule, if a country believes it is in its national interest to make a particular arms sale, it should be willing to divulge the details of the sale and provide its justification. This is particularly necessary in the case of arms transfers to human rights violators, when the possibility of misuse of weaponry is high.

Recognition of the need for disclosure, or "transparency" as it is called in the international security community, led to the establishment of the United Nations Conventional Arms Register in December 1991. The register was created to promote "transparency so as to encourage prudent restraint by states in their arms export and arms import policies and to reduce the risks of misunderstanding, suspicion or tension resulting from a lack of information."[53] Nations are requested to voluntarily submit data on their arms imports and arms exports, but only for seven categories of major weapons systems: tanks, armored vehicles, large caliber artillery systems, combat aircraft, attack helicopters, warships, and missiles and missile launchers.

Angola did not participate in the register in 1993 (the first year in which nations were requested to submit data, covering arms imports and exports that occurred in calendar year 1992), or in 1994. Of the approximately eighty nations that participated in the register last year, not a single one listed an arms transfer to Angola in 1992. This year's register data (covering 1993 arms trade) was released in mid-October 1994. Only Russia, Bulgaria, and the Czech Republic reported arms deliveries to the Angolan government. (See above for details).

Small arms and light weapons are presently not part of the Register. Human Rights Watch strongly believes that the U.N. Register should be

---

[53] U.N. Document A/46/301, Report of the Secretary-General, "Study on ways and means of promoting transparency in international transfers of conventional arms," September 9, 1991, p. 11.

expanded to include light weapons and small arms. These weapons often cause the greatest devastation to civilians.

V. VIOLATIONS OF THE LAWS OF WAR BY GOVERNMENT FORCES

The Angolan government has been responsible for widespread violations of the rules of war since the October 1992 elections, including direct attacks on civilians, indiscriminate attacks, summary executions, torture, forced displacement, and recruitment of child soldiers. Thousands of civilians have been killed or injured in the indiscriminate bombing of population centers in UNITA-controlled zones. Government forces also tortured and killed suspected UNITA supporters—civilian non-combatants—in late 1992 and early 1993.[1]

In May and June 1994, Human Rights Watch travelled and conducted interviews in Luanda, visited refugee camps near Caxito and the government-held sector of Kuito. Five days were spent in Huambo. Human Rights Watch experienced no attempts to control its work by the government and was not aware of any attempts to monitor its interviewing. However, government officials were reluctant to meet with Human Rights Watch. Several requests to speak to the Minister of Justice, Paulo Chipilica, went unanswered.

THE PURGE OF THE CITIES—OCTOBER 1992-JANUARY 1993

Luanda

Human Rights Watch interviewed twenty eyewitnesses in several of Luanda's *musseques* (poor shanty-towns) about what they had seen in October and November 1992 during the battle for Luanda. The interviews were random and were conducted in private. No translators were present. Although those interviewed in Luanda were not professed UNITA supporters, they did represent a variety of ethnic groups, including Chokwe, Bakongo, Kimbundu and Ovimbundu. UNITA cadres in Huambo were also interviewed about their experiences.

It is impossible to estimate the number killed in Luanda during the "purge," but it is probably over one thousand. Eyewitnesses Human Rights Watch met alleged they knew the locations of execution sites and mass burial

---

[1] For UNITA's public line on these events see the account of UNITA's Fátima Roque, *Angola: Em Nome da Esperança*, Bertrand Editora, Venda Nova, 1993.

61

pits in Camama, Calemba, Cidadela, in front of Miramar in the waste ground between the cliffs and the port, Neves Bendinha, and at Morro da Samba.

The government's version of events is that UNITA was trying to stage a coup d'etat and that the government responded in self-defense following uncoordinated action of civilians stirred to rage by UNITA provocations.

Following the elections, political tensions rose quickly in Luanda. On October 2, UNITA increased the number of guards around Savimbi's Luanda residence and in the following days UNITA began to take control of the zone immediately around his residence in Miramar, manning roadblocks and acting in an arrogant manner. Following the withdrawal on October 6 of UNITA's top generals from the new army (FAA) in protest of alleged election fraud, Savimbi secretly left Luanda the next day for Huambo, having refused to talk to the U.N. or Western government officials since October 3 about the deteriorating political situation.

Although Savimbi finally received U.N. Special Representative Margaret Anstee on October 9 and 10 in Huambo for discussions on the crisis, violence between UNITA and government troops and supporters continued to spread. A serious exchange of gunfire between UNITA supporters and armed police followed a car explosion in front of Luanda's Hotel Turismo. Eleven policemen were taken hostage by UNITA in the hotel, but were released later that day in exchange for thirty-five arrested UNITA members. Four people died including one civilian wearing an MPLA T-shirt. That evening there were further clashes in Luanda's suburbs of Rosa Pinto and Gamek, close to the U.N. compound at Vila Espa.

Continued clashes occurred in the build-up to the announcement of the election results on October 17, and fighting intensified following the announcement. On October 15, ammunition depots at Luanda's airport were sabotaged by UNITA, resulting in a series of enormous explosions. By October 30, with reports of UNITA advances across the country, the government responded. The government first closed the airport, alleging that UNITA had attempted to seize it. Fighting then ensued between the government's anti-riot police and UNITA forces, resulting in some casualties. Later, twelve civilians, including three Portuguese nationals, were killed in Cassenga suburb by UNITA soldiers. The government responded by setting up road blocks across the city.

Shooting continued the next day. In the morning, UNITA and government officials held an emergency meeting to discuss the escalating hostilities. They agreed to issue a statement calling on both sides to cease fighting immediately and for U.N. and Troika observation of trouble spots to take immediate effect. However, less than sixty minutes after the meeting ended, at about 2:00 p.m., major clashes broke out across the city. Anti-riot police, regular police and some apparent civilians, armed with AK-47s, RPG-7s, and mortars, engaged UNITA forces around Rádio Nacional de Angola and at UNITA residential areas and offices. Two Mi-24 Hind armed helicopters assisted the government police.

Savimbi's residence in Miramar, UNITA national headquarters in São Paulo, and the hotels (such as the Hotel Turismo) where UNITA's leaders were lodged suffered serious damage. Once fighting started these locations became the immediate focus of events, with government forces surrounding them. The clashes developed into a general purge of all suspected UNITA supporters in Luanda. UNITA defended its positions in Luanda, mostly using mortars, RPG-7s, PKMs, and AK-47s.

Margaret Anstee and British Ambassador John Flynn (whose residence Anstee had been in when the fighting broke out) eventually succeeded in obtaining an agreement on a ceasefire for 12:01 a.m. on November 2, although the situation did not stabilize immediately. Following a day of sporadic shooting and looting in wealthy suburbs such as Miramar, a three-day curfew from 7:00 p.m. to 6:00 a.m. was announced on November 3.

Eyewitnesses describe many violations of laws of war and internationally-recognized principles of human rights by both sides during the "Battle of Luanda."

I have lived in Luanda ten years. I come from Benguela and have worked at *****. I live in ***** suburb and it was there that I watched events during Luanda's days of great confusion. Luanda became increasingly tense in late October. My wife told me of seeing guns being given out by government cadres in the middle of the month to neighborhood vigilante groups. A friend of mine in one of these told me that they had been told to expect a UNITA invasion. He warned me to stay indoors as he said all people from the south were UNITA suspects. On the last day of the month the confusion happened. Shooting started at lunch time. Anybody in a UNITA shirt or a known Ovimbundu was to live no longer. That evening my friend armed with his AK came to the flat and stayed there that night. He saved my life. He said some people had reported me as a suspect and he was there to protect me. Shooting continued all night and I kept away from the window. The next day when I peeped out at my street I

counted over twenty bodies. One was a cousin of mine, no
UNITA supporter. He died because of his birth place. The
bodies were put into a Caterpillar. I'm told there are a series
of mass graves under Miramar where the dead were put.[2]
We have no love of UNITA but these Kimbundus used
UNITA as an excuse to get at us. They have been trying to
make this into a tribal war. No one challenges them. In
Luanda's confusion I lost three of my family and I had voted
for dos Santos as President. Look, see my voting card. I will
never vote again in my life.

Five other interviews in various locations across Luanda painted a
similar picture. The government had been arming local *Comités de Bairro*
groups (neighborhood organizations based on networks of informers) up to
several weeks before the fighting broke out and preparing them to strike back
against UNITA in Luanda if given the order. A major distribution of arms took
place on October 28-29. Tensions were already high and the behavior of UNITA
in Luanda in the final days of October, especially Salupeto Pena's threats,
increased them further.

One of those doing the killing, a member of one of the MPLA's
neighborhood committees, told Human Rights Watch:

We were armed and told to wait for orders. UNITA was
treating us like fools and we had increasing difficulty in
restraining our supporters. The reports from the municipalities
were not good. UNITA was making gains. It then shot up
Portuguese at the airport and sabotaged the airport arsenal.
Having watched it for three weeks, we knew we would have
to cut this snake's head before it bit us. When the orders came
to kill UNITA, we killed them. They then found they were
fools because we knew who was UNITA and what their tactics
were. We had been watching them for weeks while they
abused us.

A government official painted another version of events, saying,
"UNITA was planning to capture Luanda. Its leadership started trying to

---

[2] Human Rights Watch visited some of these locations, given directions by a series
of unrelated informants, most of them professed non-UNITA supporters.

mobilize its units and several FALA battalions were marching on us. We could not sit and let bad losers take over. So we fought back."

Paulo Chipilica became Angola's Minister of Justice in December 1992. When asked by Lisbon's *Público* newspaper about reports of the government handing out weapons to civilians in October 1992, he did not defend the government. He said that "the old system of the one party state was called people's power. I am not of the MPLA to answer for this nor to take any responsibility for the distribution of arms."[3]

Many of the prisoners taken at this time into government custody appear to have "disappeared" or to have been extrajudicially executed. Correspondent Karl Maier of *The Independent* and *Washington Post* was the first journalist to report on these events. In an article published on November 20, 1992, he wrote:

> A rotting human leg protruded from a mound of earth just 10 yards from the cemetery's cement wall, where 38 bullet holes told the story of an execution. A piece of the flag of Jonas Savimbi's opposition UNITA movement lying on the mound explained the reason for the killing.
>
> Two workers at the Camama cemetery, five miles south of Luanda, said the grave contained the bodies of two women and two men who were among at least a dozen people executed by Angolan police at the cemetery in early November as widespread fighting raged in the capital between government security forces and troops of Savimbi's National Union for the Total Independence of Angola (UNITA).
>
> "These four people were brought here and shot against the wall," said one gravedigger wearing a mask to avoid the smell. "We watched one morning as anti-riot police drove in two trucks, threw seven people tied up out of the back, and just shot them here in the cemetery...."
>
> At the cemetery south of Luanda, the trail of death continued just outside the walls. Another human leg marked the spot

---

[3] *Público* (Lisbon), May 23, 1994.

where four more people allegedly fell to police guns. AK-47 shells lay all around two graves.

The biggest mass grave was about 500 yards away. There, large patches of dried blood surrounded a giant pit where, two gravediggers said, police had gathered 30 people, executed them and bulldozed their bodies into the ground. Many of them, judging by the uniforms on the ground, were UNITA supporters.

The Angolan government has not yet reacted to the discovery of the graves, the first evidence that would support allegations that security forces participated in summary executions of UNITA soldiers and supporters. In UNITA-controlled areas, there have been allegations of similar atrocities by UNITA soldiers.

An official at the Defense Ministry's press office, who would identify himself only as Bravo, said the corpses must have been among the 500 bodies gathered by the authorities from the streets of Luanda after the fighting to avoid the outbreak of disease. When told of the bullet holes in the cemetery wall, the eyewitness accounts, the AK-47 shell casings and the pools of blood around the mass grave, he said he would look into the matter.

Most of the victims here were Ovimbundu, the ethnic group from the central highlands that forms the back-bone of political support for Savimbi's UNITA. Many of the assailants, witnesses said, were members of civilian militia that the police armed during the Nov. 1-3 battles in Luanda.

"What is going on here is tribal rivalry," said a 24-year-old teacher in the Kikolo shantytown on the northern edge of Luanda. "Anyone from the southern part of the country is suspected of being a UNITA supporter. If you are Ovimbundu, you are UNITA." The teacher, an Ovimbundu from Bié province, said he was picked up at his house on Nov. 10 and taken to the local police headquarters. "The only thing that saved me was that I had a piece of paper proving that I worked at a voting station during the elections." He said he knew five people who had been killed this month.

The teacher and other residents describe a life of terror, in which people lock themselves in their houses from dusk until morning, and armed gunmen, some in police uniforms, shoot into the air at night and go door to door hunting their victims.

"Many of us want to go back home to the south, but the police at the checkpoints will not let us," said a man in São Pedro de Bara shantytown. He said he saw several people being dragged from their homes down a dirt road before being taken to a nearby Fortaleza prison. They have not been seen since, he said.

A 35-year-old father of two from Huambo said police picked him up at 2 p.m. on Nov. 2 as he was visiting his niece's house. After telling him to remove his shoes, he said, an officer shot him with a pistol in the foot and marched him towards Fortaleza prison. But his niece knew some of the officers and persuaded them to let him go, he said.[4]

Interviewed in Huambo in May 1994, UNITA's Head of the Department of Health, Brigadier Morgado, described his experience in Luanda in October and November 1992. Injured and captured during the battle for Luanda, he was then held by the Emergency Police for three days before being transferred to the Ministry of Defense. From there he was moved to a High Security prison before being put into a hospital. He claims Cuban doctors saved his life because no Angolans dared be seen to help him.

I was initially put in a small cell with a young UNITA cadre from the Youth Wing, but he was soon moved. Initially I was not given food or drink. There was only a small hole for light in my cell. After 5:00 a.m. it became terrible because there was no ventilation. It became worse than a sauna. Seventeen

---

[4] *Washington Post*, November 20, 1992.

> UNITA people like me were held in solitary confinement. The
> toilet was a hole in the ground and I was given 1.5 liters of
> water a day. The food was rice. We were given no salt.

Captured UNITA supporters, and those who surrendered, were taken
to various prisons after these initial incidents, including those in the Ministry of
Defense, the RI-20 Barracks, and the Catete Road prison, Luanda's former
security prison. Prisoners were also held in the Cadeia do Commando Provincial
da Polícia, Cadeia da Esquadra de Rádio-Patrulha, the Cadeia das Operações,
Sambizanga police post and the Fortaleza and São Paulo prisons.

Informants have told Human Rights Watch that fellow inmates were
usually moved late at night from their cells by the authorities, normally after
their names had been read from lists. Sometimes they would hear shots shortly
afterwards, or the prisoners simply were never seen again.

Fernando Jamba, a UNITA sympathizer in Luanda, who has
subsequently changed his name for safety, escaped from a government firing
squad in the central police station by bribing his way out. However, on
November 2, he witnessed the police lining up over forty prisoners and
executing them in a yard. He told Human Rights Watch that he knew many of
the executed prisoners did not support UNITA. He described it as a "big
confusion."

Among those detained at the time were several members of four
opposition parties that had supported UNITA's allegations that the election
results had been rigged. André Kilandomoko, President of the Partido Social
Democrata Angolano (PSDA), Zeca, information secretary of the Partido
Democrático para O Progresso-Alianca Nacional de Angola (PDP-ANA), and
Paulino Pinto João, leader of the Convenção Nacional Democrática de Angola
(CNDA), were picked up and beaten by police at various locations. They and
other party leaders were released a few days later after being forced to make
anti-UNITA statements which were broadcast on television.[5]

Human Rights Watch found that lists of potential targets had been
drawn up in the suburbs. House-to-house searches were conducted and family
members who refused to divulge information on the whereabouts of their
relatives were beaten up. Several informants talked of members of their family
being killed immediately after they were discovered. Human Rights Watch saw
a video tape of a crowd of civilians, including very young boys, exulting over

---

[5] See also, Amnesty International, *Angola: Assault on the Right to Life*, August 20,
1993 (Afr 12/04/93).

a burning body, kicking it and throwing wood and cardboard over it. Although the state-run radio broadcast appeals on November 2 for the killing to stop, they continued. Some "over- enthusiastic" police were called off the streets by their superiors because of their excesses.[6]

During the first week of November 1992, executions occurred across Luanda on a regular basis; police and officers were seen directing some of the operations. A young Ninja officer became known as *"O Mais Rápido"* (The Fastest One) during this time because of his enthusiasm for executing people quickly at Catete Road prison. Prisoners were also subjected to mock executions or threatened with execution at Catete Road. Torture of UNITA prisoners taken to the Ministry of the Interior's high-security interrogation facility, Central de Criminalística, known as the "Laboratório," at Catete Road also occurred. By mid-November these abuses had become more sporadic. However, sweeps in which people "disappeared" continued. In May 1994 Human Rights Watch interviewed a family in Samba suburb who believed their son was killed by police because they originated from the planalto.

UNITA supporters were not the only ones targeted in this period. On Friday, January 22, 1993 a week of violence broke out in Luanda against Zairian residents. *Jeune Afrique* reports:

> The entire city had become a hunting ground. Hunting for Zairenses, that is to say for Zairians and assimilated individuals. Early on Friday morning January 22, bands armed with machetes, pistols and Kalashnikovs (AK-47s) invaded the main market, well-known to accommodate the Zairians. During four hours they looted the vendor stalls, overturning booths, wrecking the sheds and raping women and adolescents. The only slogan: "Basta desses Zairenses!" (Enough of these Zairians!). The police had miraculously disappeared.
>
> All of the markets considered to be occupied by the Zairians suffered the same fate. The Kwanzas Market in the Mabor neighborhood. The Congolese Market in the neighborhood of

---

[6] There were exceptions. UNITA's General Ben-Ben was assisted by a government soldier in his escape from Luanda (see *Expresso*, September 11, 1993) and not all Ovimbundus were targeted. Indeed, Ovimbundus remain important in the local Luanda economy for their market gardening in the suburbs.

the "Prophet" Simão Toco. Even at Mutamba, the administrative downtown area. A youngster was killed. His crime? He sells cigarettes. Consequently, he is Zairian. At night, during the two nights of horror, the Zairian neighborhoods became torture camps. Palanca of course, but also Hoji-ya-Henda, Kikolo, Mabor, Petrangol, Rocha Pinto, Samba, Viana...[7]

The official figure for those killed in these disturbances, which are now commonly known as "Bloody Friday," is sixty-nine. These attacks against Zairians in fact occurred while UNITA was making significant gains in Angola's northern Bakongo provinces of Zaire and Uíge. Rádio Nacional de Angola had broadcast a story about the alleged arrival of Zairian commandos to assassinate President dos Santos and allegations that Zairian troops assisted UNITA in assaults on Soyo and Huambo.

Two weeks after "Bloody Friday," the Angolan government finally issued a condemnation of the killings. Nearly a year later, on January 11, 1994, a parliamentary commission of inquiry conducted by thirteen members of the National Assembly absolved the government of all responsibility for "Bloody Friday," concluding that the violence was a "spontaneous demonstration without any tribal essence or basis." According to the inquiry, those responsible were policemen, civilians and soldiers who had fled Soyo following UNITA's occupation of that oil center. Minister of the Interior Santana André Pitra "Petroff" informed the commission that the courts were dealing with twenty-five cases of people allegedly involved in "Bloody Friday."

Human Rights Watch's investigation of this incident among eyewitnesses and survivors suggests that more than sixty-nine people were killed. Moreover, there is credible evidence that the Luanda authorities deliberately turned a blind eye on events initially and could have intervened on January 22 if they had so wished. It also does not appear that soldiers from Soyo were the protagonists. Most withdrew to Luanda from the Soyo area on January 17-18 and only arrived in Luanda after "Bloody Friday."

Lubango

The purge of UNITA was not limited to Luanda. Violence also erupted in Lubango. António, a UNITA sympathizer, described events:

---

[7] *Jeune Afrique*, March 4, 1993.

> Things got bad for me after October 1992. I lived in Lubango and had a business there. My house got mortared three times in November, destroying much of what I owned. Finally after my brother warned me I left and hid in a river. On January 6, the Ninjas came and looted and destroyed my house. I fled to Quilengues and from there have moved to Caluquembe. I now try and make business for the party. I have not heard any news about my family since those events.

In January 1993, the UNAVEM II delegation in Lubango tried to restore peace but its efforts failed after government police entered the UNAVEM compound and arrested three UNITA members of the joint government-UNITA monitoring commission set up under the Peace Accords who had sought refuge in the camp. One of them was killed on the spot; the other two were taken away despite UNAVEM protests. They have not been seen alive since.

Sérgio, also a UNITA sympathizer, described the situation in Lubango in January. He had moved into UNITA's stronghold in the Hotel Imperio because his house had been destroyed by vigilante groups in early November.

> On January 2 some forty Ninjas moved up on us at the Hotel Império. Some of those Ninjas used a T-55 tank to shoot two shells at us. There were over 300 people in the hotel, mostly civilian members of the party and no warning was given. The Ninjas then cut off access to the hotel. Then on January 3 they just randomly shot at the hotel. At the same time they purged Lubango further of any suspected supporters. They had lists drawn up of houses and locations to be attacked. Inspector João Alberto "Do Do" of the Ninjas directed the operations. He had arrived in city after Bicesse from Luanda. The majority of the killings were done by Ninjas brought in from Luanda. Local Ninjas attempted to avoid direct action and many local people refused to assist. Hotel room 305 in which twenty-five children were staying for their safety is an example of their lack of mercy. Dynamite sticks were thrown in. All the children died immediately or later because of their wounds. One of mine too.

Reporter Karl Maier interviewed a doctor in Lubango who witnessed government soldiers enter the Hotel Imperio, execute one teenager and force another to lie on the ground as they emptied four AK-47 assault rifles into him. "His body danced with death until it became like jelly," the doctor said.[8] Amnesty International estimates that over 200 suspected UNITA supporters were extrajudicially executed in Lubango between January 1 and 4 by police and armed civilians.[9]

Lobito and Benguela

Lobito suffered from waves of violence in November 1992 and again in January 1993. In November the damage was heaviest in the center of town, where Ninja police, armed pro-government vigilantes (Fitinhas), and other looters ransacked many buildings. Jorge da Cruz was based in Lobito as UNITA's representative on the National Electoral Council (CNE). He now works for UNITA's Foreign Affairs department. He told Human Rights Watch:

> After Luanda we had our problems in Lobito in early November up to November 3. The Ninjas shelled us in the Hotel Gran Tosco with a T-55 tank. They also used AK-47s and RPG-7s against us. Ninjas and armed civilians killed various of our supporters, while others were detained and we have heard no more of them. The U.N. negotiations which resulted in the Namibe agreement gave us a lull. But the government in December was sending more Ninjas to build up their forces. Then on January 5 fighting became fierce. The Ninjas used T-55s and the Navy to bombard the hotel. On January 5 and 6 we fought back, but on January 7 we withdrew through four ambushes. Once the Ninjas had destroyed UNITA's official presence they set on innocent civilians who had nothing to do with this conflict. The police encouraged mob rule.

Many innocent people suffered in Lobito and Benguela during this second purge of UNITA in January. Human Rights Watch interviewed over twenty people who had fled from these cities at that time. Each of them talked

---

[8] *The Independent on Sunday* (London), September 31, 1993.

[9] Amnesty International, *Angola: Assault on the Right to Life*, August 20, 1993.

of an incident in which suspected UNITA supporters were rounded up and locked into a container where they died of heat exhaustion and suffocation. UNITA alleges that the container was near the Alto Boque park on the road to Benguela. This has become a much-repeated story of government brutality amongst UNITA supporters.

Human Rights Watch interviewed a government supporter who had a different version of the story. He described how he and his friends "culled UNITAs in Lobito" during the purge. He said that he had heard that over fifty UNITAs were put in a cargo container and then killed when a RPG-7 projectile was fired inside the container, but he denied they were civilians.

Foreign journalists who visited Lobito and Benguela later in January 1993 estimate over 1,000 people were killed in the week of fighting, or *"Limpeza"* (cleansing), against UNITA. A U.S. government official has put the toll as high as 3,500.[10] An eyewitness told *Guardian* correspondent Chris McGreal that in Catumbela, "They gave the children guns, some aged only twelve or thirteen. The police showed people where the homes of the UNITA supporters were. A lot of people here were killed. How many died, I can't say."[11]

Other Cities

A similar pattern of violence against UNITA emerged across the country. This is one former policeman's account:

> I'm from Malanje. Confusion came to us on the day it came
> to Luanda. When we heard of events in Luanda we acted too.
> We pushed those UNITAs out. They had caused us too much
> work. Many died and we captured some too. Gravediggers
> worked hard the next day as we only kept those we wanted.
> The others died, but I had nothing to do with this. Look what
> has happened to us. Our life is war and I don't want any more
> children because there is no future for us.

---

[10] James Woods, Deputy Assistant Secretary of Defense for African Affairs, in "The Quest for Peace in Angola," Hearing before the Subcommittee on Africa of the House Foreign Affairs Committee (Washington: U.S. Government Printing Office), November 16, 1993, p. 8.

[11] *The Guardian* (London), January 18, 1993.

António, a UNITA supporter from Kuito, described what happened to him on January 6. He is thirty-nine and a father of three. He was born in Kuito and was interviewed by Human Rights Watch in Huambo. His family owned a series of shops in Kuito.

> I have lived in Kuito much of my life and support UNITA. The MPLA murdered my brother in 1990 and a cousin in November 1992. We are known UNITA sympathizers. I have worked for over ten years for the movement. Things were already bad in Kuito and my family was divided in its allegiance. Some of my cousins and a sister support the MPLA. I stayed as long as I dared but my relatives warned me that the commander of the Ninjas had been ordered to purge all UNITA sympathizers from the town. Then I knew it as real war and fled. I joined other family and am now with UNITA fully. On January 6 over twenty people were picked up by those Ninjas. We don't know what happened to them. I believe they were killed. Most of them were innocents, their crime was blood ties to UNITA supporters. But how can that be a crime. Kuito is divided; divided families, divided loyalties. It is less of a fight for ideology than a fight of families. The feud has a long history.

UNITA was successfully pushed out of Kuito on January 10 and the pro-government forces commenced to loot the city, breaking into shops, homes, and government buildings, taking anything they could carry while the authorities watched helplessly.

Government forces ousted UNITA from its urban foot-holds in Sumbe in December 1992; Lucapa, Dundo (Lunda Norte) and Saurimo (Lunda Sul) on January 7; Huambo and Menongue (Kuando Kubango) on January 9; and Luena (Moxico) on January 10, 1993.

CONTINUING ABUSES IN 1993 AND 1994

Quilengues—Summary Executions On the Front Line
Some of the worst government abuses have occurred immediately after ground forces newly capture territory from UNITA. In Huambo, Human Rights Watch interviewed several people who had fled from Quilengues (Huíla) in the

second half of August 1993. Among these was Maria, age sixty-three, whose husband was killed by government special forces which entered the town before the main army on August 19:

> It was early in the morning and I was in bed with my husband when we woke and heard shooting. Government forces had entered the town and were shooting into the houses. My husband, Garcia, is a UNITA supporter and businessman, not a soldier, and he ran out of the house to help our forces. He was shot at the door although he was unarmed. I heard the shot and his grunt so ran out of the back door. I then watched the soldiers shoot up my house before they set it on fire and moved on.
>
> A group of people were taken to the front of the UNITA delegation office and executed. They were the senior people in the town, mostly traders and party officials, killed as a warning to the others not to support UNITA. I heard the shots, but did not see what actually happened. I then decided it was too dangerous to stay and joined a group of fleeing residents. Many people died that morning. I saw the bodies of José Maria, Raimundo, and Beto Poeiras in a street before I fled out of town. People have told me that over 200 people died that day. But I didn't see this.

Huambo—Bombs, Mines, Children, and Human Shields

On March 6, 1993, after fifty-five days of UNITA siege of the city of Huambo (see below), government forces retreated to Benguela, with tens of thousands of civilians fleeing with them. To defend the flank of its retreating troops from hot pursuit by UNITA, the government dropped a carpet of antipersonnel mines in Huambo's San Antonio suburb. Women and children appear to have been forced to stay at the rear of the retreating troops to act as human shields. One eyewitness told Human Rights Watch that during the final days of the siege, "Children nine or ten years old were brought in to shoot at UNITA."

UNITA's military Chief of Staff, General Arlindo Pena "Ben-Ben" described the siege of Huambo and subsequent events in the following terms: "Huambo had more civilian casualties than any other type, because of the [government's] use of the Air Force. The military men—MPLA troops and our troops—were fighting very close, so the Air Force avoided bombing there and bombed residential areas instead. I think the overall toll, civilian and military, is over 12,000."[12]

Kuito—Killing for Food

The desperation for food during the battle for Kuito (see below) was so acute that Human Rights Watch obtained testimonies from women who had been forced by government officers to go into "no man's land" to collect parachute-dropped supplies intended for them, but which had missed their target. A woman related the following:

> A few weeks ago [May 1994] when parachutes came down, José, a Ninja, ordered that I and some others go into the bush to pick up some supplies for them. UNITA did not cause my injury but government soldiers, they fired at me and then at the police who fired back. A lot of confusion followed. Two civilians were killed and the others are in the hospital.

Human Rights Watch visited the hospital. A government official told us that all hospital patients with gunshot wounds were casualties caused by UNITA. Interviews conducted later in private established that the majority of the injured were from this gunfight between the government's own police and army over parachute supplies. According to the medical staff at the hospital, fighting also starts when government soldiers sneak into UNITA-held territory to retrieve supplies of foodstuffs, cigarettes and ammunition dropped from high altitude parachute drops. Even when the drops hit their target, they provoke clashes among government soldiers and police. In an attempt to reduce this squabbling, parachute drops for the police and army are made on different days. But residents say they have seen little improvement. When UNITA is not shelling, and humanitarian aid is not suspended, exchanges of fire between different government military groups are the single greatest cause of civilian casualties.

Malanje—Cutting Off the Hands of Children

A similar situation exists in Malanje. Lawlessness between different government security forces in the city can be acute. An Angolan resident of Malanje who had successfully fled to Luanda described the city as having six different security forces operating there. He described them as, "Fubus, Gatos,

---

[12] *Jane's Defence Weekly*, June 5, 1993.

FAA, FAPLA, Ninjas, and regular police. They all fight for food and those who do not have guns suffer."

Several relief workers have witnessed children caught stealing food having their hands cut off by officials as punishment. Diversion of food aid to soldiers in Malanje is also a serious problem. Malanje's governor, Flávio Fernandes, is named by many former residents of the city as one of the main culprits. Reportedly, on his orders supplies have been flown back to Luanda to be sold in the markets there or diverted at Luanda before they even get on the flight to Malanje.

According to observers, Fernandes tried to dismiss Conceiçáo Araújo, Malanje director of the government relief agency Minars, after she levelled corruption charges against him, but she refused to go. Prime Minister Marcelino Moco flew in to settle the dispute and Araujo was transferred to Bengo province. The U.S. government has tried to put pressure on Luanda to remove Fernandes, even ordering that no U.S. food aid be sent to Malanje, but Fernandes remains in power.

INDISCRIMINATE BOMBING AND SHELLING

In November 1992 the government began systematic bombing of UNITA-held towns despite the fact that many contained significant concentrations of civilians. Its aircraft often fly at high altitude and do not attempt to pinpoint their targets. High explosive 150 and 200 kilogram bombs have been used in these raids. U.N. and other officials have confirmed that cluster bombs have been widely used, and with increasing frequency.

According to these officials and other observers, there is also credible evidence that phosphorus bombs have been used. Human Rights Watch has not been able to confirm conclusively the use of phosphorus bombs against the civilian population, but believes that this issue deserves greater scrutiny and investigation. In addition, Human Rights Watch interviewed several eyewitnesses but was unable to confirm UNITA's allegations that fuel-air explosive bombs, napalm, and chemical weapons are being used in the government's offensives in Lunda Norte and Sul and in the Zaire, Uíge and Cuanza Norte operations.[13]

---

[13] For many years UNITA has alleged that the government is using chemical weapons. A review of the literature on this subject can be found in Elaine Windrich, *The Cold War Guerrilla: Jonas Savimbi, the U.S. Media, and the Angolan War* (New York: Greenwood, 1992), pp. 95-104. See also, Brian Davey, "Chemical Warfare in Angola?,"

While it is impossible to determine the precise targets of much of the government's bombing and shelling attacks, Human Rights Watch's investigations did reveal that suburbs where civilians are the predominant residents have been extensively hit. All localities under UNITA control appear to have been regarded as potential targets.

The following is a sample of the incidents in which Human Rights Watch has confirmed that civilians and their properties suffered severely from government bombing or rocket attacks. Human Rights Watch inspected sites of rocket and bomb damage in Huambo in May 1994. Several instances Human Rights Watch witnessed of damage to civilian property were probably misses of designated targets, as they were located near the airport or near housing for UNITA's senior leadership. Other instances of damage to civilian property were clearly caused by random and indiscriminate shelling and bombing attacks. All interviews were with civilians. People interviewed usually called all bombers MiGs, although their descriptions often indicated that the planes were Su-22s.

● February 8, 1993   Chiva suburb

A rocket killed two people, one a child called João Batista.
Another rocket injured nine people and killed one. A 13-year-old called Matinez was blinded. He told the tale:

> It was during the battle for Huambo. Suddenly a rocket exploded in the kitchen where I was hiding. There was a flash, an explosion and then the roof came down on top of me. I have not been able to see since. I know when it's day and night but no more.

Human Rights Watch was also shown an unexploded Russian-manufactured 250 kilogram bomb upside down and sticking out of an old woman's front porch. It was one of four bombs dropped nearby. Two of her neighbors were killed. Local people said that thirty were killed and sixty-seven injured in the suburb that day from government bombing. No soldiers had been in the vicinity as this was a residential area, away from the front line.

UNITA's capture of Huambo in March did not end aerial bombings by the government.

Jane's Intelligence Review, June 1993, pp. 280-283.

• Justino is a fifty-year-old Ovimbundu from Huambo. He and his family had fled from Huambo in early January 1993 as fighting intensified. He then returned to the city in July when he decided it was safe. At 10:00 a.m. on August 8, a MiG dropped four bombs. His house was completely destroyed.

• António is thirty-nine. His cousin and two children were killed when a MiG dropped four bombs on August 21. His hut was destroyed completely and he was hospitalized for thirty days.

• Maria was at the Central Hospital when a rocket from a MiG hit nearby on August 26. She was slightly injured. Human Rights Watch inspected fragments near the point of impact, and believes it was a Brazilian SBAT-70 2M, like the unexploded rocket mentioned earlier that UNITA found nearby.

• Human Rights Watch inspected the site where four bombs dropped by a Su-22 landed in Huambo on 11:22 a.m. on February 7, 1994. Two houses were destroyed, a seven-year-old child was killed and three adults injured by what appears to have been four 150 kilogram bombs. None of the bombs landed anywhere near a military target. UNITA claimed at the time that seventy-six people died. This could not be confirmed and appears to be an exaggeration. Angolan Presidential spokesman, Aldmiro da Conceiçáo, was interviewed by Portuguese RDP-1 radio about this raid:

> [Da Conceiçáo] "As we have stated several times before, Huambo is an area of conflict and as such it is subject to the vicissitudes of war, air strikes included.
> [RDP reporter Walter Medeiros] But do you bomb indiscriminately?
> [A] Obviously we aim at military targets, and we know where the troops are deployed at present in Huambo.[14]

However, this simply does not appear to be the case. The bombs struck a densely populated suburb of mud huts. The aircraft had dropped them from an altitude too high to allow for precise targeting.

The International Committee of the Red Cross (ICRC) has also suffered from poor targeting by the government Air Force. On August 4, 1993 the ICRC

---

[14] RDP Antena-1 Radio, Lisbon, in Portuguese, 2100 gmt, February 8, 1994.

issued one of its rare press releases, which indicates the seriousness of the incident:

> Huambo has been under heavy air attack by government armed forces since 2 August, causing an unknown number of casualties. Several areas of the town, including those inhabited by civilians, continue to be bombarded.
>
> At 10 am local time on 4 August the ICRC delegation was hit by bombs and completely destroyed. By miracle the delegate and local employees escaped injury. The building was duly marked with the Red Cross Emblem.
>
> The ICRC urgently appeals to the belligerents to comply with the Rules of International Humanitarian Law concerning the civilian population, the wounded, detainees and the Red Cross emblem.[15]

Non-governmental organizations (NGOs) and U.N. agencies in Huambo confirmed eleven bombing incidents there between January and late April 1994. Then, after a lull, the government embarked on a renewed aerial bombing campaign on the city. NGOs report that between May 29 and June 5 over twenty high explosive and incendiary bombs were dropped on Huambo, hitting the airport, São João, São José and Cacilhas suburbs. On June 3, two Su-22s reportedly dropped eight phosphorus bombs at 11:04 a.m. and 1:34 p.m.

Human Rights Watch interviewed several people who had recently witnessed government bombing in other locations.

• José is a 45-year-old UNITA logistics man based at Kalukembe. He was in Huambo on business. He told how six bombs landed in the central square in March 1994 while trade was going on. Sixteen people were killed. He believed that one of the bombs was a phosphorus bomb, and the others were cluster bombs. He said, "Children don't go to school. They stay in bunkers and come out at dusk when danger is over."

---

[15] ICRC Press Release No.93/24. The government subsequently issued a public apology but claimed that UNITA's General Staff was housed in a building close to the ICRC and was using the ICRC's facilities as a shield.

• João was in Bailumbo in February. He saw ten 150 kilogram bombs dropped by Su-22s. His son, a three-year-old, was killed. He said:

> The planes fly very high. We live outside the town for safety
> and come into it to trade. The planes come from the direction
> of Catumbela. Phosphorus bombs are a big problem. We all
> carry water and a cloth. If the bombs drop we can dip this
> cloth into the water and put it across our face as a filter.
> That's life for us these days.

The government has several times called for more discipline in the Air Force, but only in the context of better maintenance of equipment. For example, on January 15, 1994, General João de Matos, Chief of Staff of the Angolan Armed Forces, stated, "The Air Force should continue to aim its activities at the training and upgrading of its cadres, and increased military discipline of its personnel to prevent the loss of technical means and weaponry as these cost our country dearly."[16] Respect for the international laws of war does not seem to be a consideration.

The government has also mistakenly bombed civilians in its own zones. On June 6 at 12:20 p.m., a government fighter aircraft dropped bombs over Waku Kungo, hitting a school, killing eighty-nine students and wounding many others. Other buildings were badly damaged and several hundred other people injured. The Air Force held an internal investigation. Its conclusion was that the aircraft misjudged its position because of a misreading in its course indicator and because visual observation was hampered by thick fog, putting it 40 to 50 kilometers off course.[17]

The government has used its air raids on airports and airstrips in UNITA-controlled territory to force the suspension of international relief efforts in these areas.

UNITA alleged that M-46 artillery, and other long-range, self-propelled artillery pieces, as well as T-55 and T-62 tanks, were used to shell Ndalatando indiscriminately before it was recaptured by the government in late April 1994.

---

[16] Rádio Nacional de Angola, Luanda, in Portuguese, 0600 gmt, January 15, 1994.

[17] Communique on incident issued by the General Staff of the Angolan Armed Forces on June 9, 1994, broadcast on Rádio Nacional de Angola, Luanda, in Portuguese, 2034 gmt, June 9, 1994.

Human Rights Watch attempted to visit Ndalatando in May to assess these allegations but the government would not assist in setting up a visit.

Applicable Legal Standards

Many of the bombing attacks described above were indiscriminate and violated the rules of war.[18] Indiscriminate attacks are defined in Article 51 (4) of Protocol I to the Geneva Conventions, as:

> a) those which are not directed at a specific military objective;

> b) those which employ a method or means of combat which cannot be directed at a specific military objective; or

> c) those which employ a method or means of combat the effects of which cannot be limited as required by this Protocol; and consequently, in each such case, are of a nature to strike military objectives and civilians or civilian objects without distinction.

A further definition of indiscriminate attacks is in Protocol I, Article 51 (5) (b), referring to those attacks which may be expected to cause incidental loss of civilian life, injury to civilians, damage to civilian objects, or a combination thereof, which would be excessive in relation to the concrete and direct military advantage anticipated. This codifies the rule of proportionality: an attack which may be expected to cause excessive casualties and damage is a disproportionate attack. The rule reflects a balance between 1) the foreseeable extent of incidental ("collateral") civilian casualties or damage, and 2) the relative importance of the military objective as a target. No matter what the value of the military objective, it never justifies excessive civilian casualties.

The government has defended its position. When interviewed by Human Rights Watch in May, Vice-Minister for Defense General Pedro Sebastião commented, "We don't waste our money bombing civilians." Eyewitness accounts given to Human Rights Watch, as well as those given to U.N. and NGO staff, refute this claim.

The pattern of many aerial bombings suggests that although the government may not have been engaging in the forbidden practice of deliberately targeting civilians, it was nevertheless engaging in the practice of using a means

---

[18] See Chapter Eight for a detailed discussion.

of attack which was not capable of being directed at a military target. Such attacks (e.g. those employing a "method or means of combat which cannot be directed at a specific military objective") are forbidden under the rules of war.

The method used by the Angolan Air Force has been described time and again as bombing from very high altitudes. In practice, this method of attack has been indiscriminate. Whether through incapacity to accurately target, or the failure even to attempt to do so, these high altitude raids have persistently devastated civilian objects and areas. There are many accounts of bombs landing kilometers away from known military targets. In the case of the bombings in Huambo, bombs apparently aimed at the airport landed over a kilometer away in surrounding suburbs.

Where the military target is in a non-populated area, a lack of targeting capability would not be a barrier to bombing. If the government uses bombing systems that have no apparent targeting mechanisms in populated areas, it is clearly engaged in indiscriminate bombing. It is the duty of the attacker to take reasonable precautions to avoid inflicting excessive civilian casualties, and to refrain from attack if such avoidance is not possible.

Non-military government officials have responded to Human Rights Watch that UNITA concentrates civilians as human shields and that these are therefore legitimate targets. Whatever UNITA's strategy, it can never be an excuse for the government to launch attacks which will cause excessive civilian casualties. Even if UNITA deliberately locates bases in the immediate proximity to civilian concentrations, under the rules of war the government must still adhere to the rule of proportionality and either use precision weapons as a necessary precaution to avoid such casualties, or, if it does not have the means to avoid such civilian harm, refrain from attack.

Finally, several of the attacks described above—on market places for example—do not appear to have been directed at a specific military objective. Civilians and civilian objectives are not legitimate objectives and they may not be directly targeted.

TORTURE AND MISTREATMENT OF PRISONERS

Captured UNITA prisoners are often held in inhuman conditions. Many prisons, lacking adequate financial support from the government, are unable to supply prisoners with food and medicine. The prisoners are therefore forced to depend on outside help, particularly their families. UNITA detainees often did not receive assistance and several told us they were given a liter of dirty water and some spoonfuls of rice a day on which to survive. The International Committee of the Red Cross estimates that there are some 1,100 UNITA detainees in Luanda.

In the besieged cities or on the fronts UNITA soldiers were often extrajudicially executed after interrogation. After the government recaptured Soyo on March 12, 1993 an army officer in the city told a journalist that "there are very few prisoners of war" there.[19] In Kuito, NGO workers said they had never heard of long-term prisoners, since food was short and no place was secure enough to hold prisoners for long periods of time.

Photographs by Jack Pecone published in September 1993 in the London *Observer* showed government soldiers beating up a suspected UNITA spy.[20] Pecone wrote:

> A group of MPLA government soldiers had discovered the man in a village outside Ganda, southern Angola. After chasing him through the dusty red streets, they grabbed him by the shirt and spun him around. Then he was slapped and shoved and sent flying into the scrub. He was pulled up, kicked in the face and punched. Then one soldier raised his rifle butt and smashed it into the man's head. Others followed.
>
> As he staggered, blood pouring from his head, another shot his feet—a routine treatment of prisoners. A few more shots left him unconscious in the midday sun.

FORCED DISPLACEMENT

Forced displacement of the civilian population for reasons connected with a conflict is prohibited under Article 17, Protocol II, which makes only two exceptions: the immediate safety of the civilians and imperative military reasons.[21]

---

[19] Amnesty International, *Angola: Assault on the Right to Life*.

[20] *The Observer* (London), September 5, 1993.

[21] Protocol II, Article 17 states: "The displacement of the civilian population shall not be ordered for reasons related to the conflict unless the security of the civilians involved or imperative military reasons so demand. Should such displacements have to

The term "imperative military reasons" usually refers to evacuation in the face of imminent military operations. Evacuation is appropriate if an area is in danger as a result of military operations or is liable to be subjected to military operations such as intense bombing. It may also be permitted when the presence of protected persons in an area hampers military operations. The prompt return of the evacuees to their homes is required as soon as hostilities in the area have ceased. (See Chapter Eight).

Witnesses told Human Rights Watch how the government ordered people to flee their homes and move to resettlement areas in August 1993. Eduardo (age forty-five), a father of three from Porto Quipiri, told of army soldiers twice ordering his family to flee without being allowed to take their possessions, first on November 1, 1992 and then in August 1993, when UNITA units were operating again in the area. All possessions he left behind were looted. UNITA entered Porto Quipiri on November 2. Eduardo has since been able to return to his home but found that UNITA had destroyed everything. UNITA did the same in the nearby provincial capital of Caxito, wrecking anything associated with the government when it entered the city in November 1992. The offices of the national bank, interior ministry and governor's palace were all destroyed.

CHILD SOLDIERS

Underage recruitment and use of child soldiers is a widespread problem. Under the rules of war, recruitment, voluntary or involuntary, of soldiers under the age of fifteen is illegal.[22] Human Rights Watch witnessed teenagers being picked up by soldiers late at night in Luanda in Samba suburb and Ilha de Luanda. Many families try to keep their teenage sons off the streets in an attempt to keep them from being grabbed.

One fourteen-year-old who had been seized by the army in Luanda in January 1994 and taken to fight in Ndalatando said:

---

may be received under satisfactory conditions of shelter, hygiene, health, safety and nutrition." See Chapter Eight.

[22] Protocol II, Article 4 (3) (c): "Children who have not attained the age of fifteen years shall neither be recruited in the armed forces or groups nor allowed to take part in hostilities."

I was talking with some friends by the road when a lorry stopped and some soldiers jumped out and grabbed us. The back of the lorry had some twenty other young people, all taken like me. We were then driven out to a camp past Caxito and given military training. I spent February learning how to fire a gun before being made to go to the front line near Ndalatando. When I could I escaped and came back to Luanda. Although I told people I was fourteen and showed the officials my identity document, they never listened. There were many like me.

Rounding up of forced recruits in this manner is commonplace. There are credible reports of a similar pattern in Benguela, Lobito and Lubango. Refugee camps for the internally displaced are favorite targets for forced recruitment. José, a displaced person from Zala (Cuanza Norte) said, "Friday and Saturday nights the lorries stop [at the Boa Esperança refugee camp]. You wonder who will be next. All our young men are being taken."

Boa Esperança holds a group of Katangan refugees from Zaire under protection of the United Nations High Commissioner for Refugees (UNHCR). They should be doubly protected, but the forced recruitment squads snatch these young men, too. At 5:00 a.m. on May 20, 1994, six young Katangans were snatched and taken to Viana police station. Two were freed but the whereabouts of the others remains unknown; possibly they have been put into the government's Katangan regiment based at Viana. The missing men are Mwangala-Jean, Kabeya-Ikole, Tshiwewe-Kamanda, and Diur-Jean-Mari. Tehibamba-Remy, the coordinator of the Zairian refugees, pleaded, "This is not our war. We are under UNHCR protection but they do nothing to help us. We would rather go home than stay here and lose our young to a war which we have no business with."

In September 1994, a trainer from Executive Outcomes told the Johannesburg *Weekly Mail and Guardian* that his problems in training the FAA "included FAA obtaining its recruits by commandeering boys as young as eight for training." He said EO tried to weed out those younger than sixteen.[23]

Human Rights Watch saw a child soldier in Kuito who appeared to be no older than ten and photographed him. When shown the photo in July during a meeting with Human Rights Watch, MPLA Information Secretary João Lourenco conceded that recruitment of children was possible. He justified it by

---

[23] *The Weekly Mail and Guardian* (Johannesburg), September 16-22, 1994.

saying, "The people in Kuito and Malanje and other besieged cities are fighting for their survival. Everybody has to fight. Young, old, even the sick. But they volunteer. Otherwise they would be killed by UNITA." No such exception is permitted under the rules of war and the Convention on the Rights of the Child. Underage recruitment is a violation of the government's obligations and duties to children.

VI. VIOLATIONS OF THE LAWS OF WAR BY UNITA FORCES

UNITA has been guilty of horrendous violations of the laws of war, including direct attacks on civilians, indiscriminate shelling, summary executions, mutilation of corpses, starvation of civilians, hostage-taking, forced portering, recruitment of child soldiers, denial of the freedom of movement, and blockage of relief aid.

The May-June 1994 mission was Human Rights Watch's first visit to a UNITA-controlled zone. Although UNITA facilitated the visit, it attempted to control the interviewing tightly by producing all the interviewees and an escort from its Department of Foreign Affairs. The escort refused to leave meetings when requested. Human Rights Watch formally complained but was told by UNITA's Minister for Social Assistance and Human Rights, Boris Mandombe, that the escort was only a "guide." UNITA's approach meant that Human Rights Watch had to disregard a significant amount of the interview material because of the compromised situation in which it was conducted. However, several opportunities arose in Huambo to conduct interviews in confidential conditions free of UNITA scrutiny.

UNITA's Governor of Huambo, Jeronimo Elavoko Wanga, who claimed he was the movement's Prime Minister, told Human Rights Watch during a meeting in Huambo in May that UNITA has a respectable human rights record. He stated:

> We follow all international conventions. Copies of the Geneva conventions are distributed to our front line troops. We agree with Amnesty International about capital punishment. We believe in humanity. Political and military prisoners are also treated in this manner. Our FALA system is based on solidarity with the people. The people give to our forces voluntarily. We don't need to use force and don't. In civilian areas, civil authorities control. We now have civilian police who are distinguished by their arm bands. We don't have the resources for uniforms yet. Our Ministry of Justice is building up the legal system again. Within forty-eight hours of detention the case must be brought before the tribunal and a lawyer present.

Human Rights Watch observed a radically different picture of UNITA's conduct in this conflict.

THE CITY SIEGES

Huambo

An estimated 10,000 people died in the battle for Huambo, many of them civilians. There were a few of days of skirmishes in October 1992, and by November 20 was the city was effectively divided, with UNITA troops controlling most of the city, while the government held the center around MPLA party headquarters and the abandoned governor's palace. Governor Baltazar had fled the week before to Luanda, and never returned.

In January 1993, the first serious fighting broke out. On January 8, government forces inside the central city attacked UNITA positions around the city limits. Jonas Savimbi's house was destroyed. UNITA forces were evicted from their key positions after two days of fierce fighting. UNITA counter-attacked and regained a foothold in the northern suburbs of the city, but was then repulsed under waves of air attacks on January 12. Several hundred people were killed in this initial fighting.

UNITA then laid siege to the city, shelling it with long-range artillery. The government returned fire and its Air Force bombed suspected UNITA positions. On some days, UNITA was reported to have fired as many as 1,000 shells into the city center. In its final stages, the siege became a combination of modern urban warfare, with street fighting between the Ninjas and UNITA forces commanded by its few urban specialists, and conventional warfare involving thousands of soldiers. In early March, UNITA soldiers overran government trenches and breached their defensive positions. Government forces were pushed back into a series of small enclaves around the governor's palace and other strategic locations. Fierce hand-to-hand combat occurred in some suburbs as UNITA advanced.

Many civilians fled from town or into the government enclaves as UNITA made its final assaults. Government soldiers held on as long as possible in the hope that two relief columns sent from the coast in mid-February would reach Huambo in time. However, UNITA forces managed to delay the government convoys by mining the single road and sniping from hills. In this fashion, UNITA prevented food, ammunition and reinforcements from reaching the city. On March 6, 1993, after fifty-five days of siege, government forces finally made a complete strategic retreat to Benguela, with tens of thousands of civilians fleeing with them.

Retreat from Huambo—Summary Executions

The retreat itself was dangerous for civilians. José Maria was in Huambo and fled when UNITA captured the city. He is now in Luanda. He describes what happened:

> Everything was destroyed. Most buildings had been hit by shells or bombs from the MiGs. We were very short of food and water and the soldiers were very tired. In the last weeks the dead were left in the streets because it was too dangerous to bury them. But things became much worse for us on our escape from Huambo. It is true that UNITA let us out of Huambo, but it was like a cat with a mouse. It played with us before the kill. We were mostly civilians in my group, some six hundred strong, but seventy of our people were killed by UNITA before we reached safety. UNITA attacked us three times. Anybody they caught, they killed, punishing them for trying to leave. They like killing too much.

T.L. was with a group of around 1,000 people in late February before the fall of Huambo. Close to Ganda, about sixty miles west of Huambo, UNITA attacked them. Ten people were killed in the shooting and the displaced scattered, hiding where they could in the bush. UNITA then swooped in and captured the injured, including some women. Possibly aware that they were being watched, UNITA soldiers organized a series of public executions. T.L. describes what he saw:

> They put a friend of mine, Miguel Dias, down on a piece of wood and chopped his head off with a machete. He had been a FAA soldier, but was unarmed, although in a tattered uniform. Three people were killed in this manner. Some of the badly injured were thrown into a river to drown. We escaped when it was dark and the Savimbis had moved on.

Semana de Loucura (Crazy Week)

For the many people who decided not to flee Huambo when UNITA occupied it, the situation deteriorated significantly. Ten days of anarchy followed which were from all accounts more damaging than the fifty-five-day siege itself. Jorge, a soldier, was in Huambo's central hospital with a bullet wound when

UNITA entered the city. He told Human Rights Watch about the moment UNITA entered the city.

> The military and civilian wounded were mixed and many civilians had moved to the hospital hoping that UNITA would respect it as a neutral location. When UNITA entered the hospital they divided the walking wounded from those too ill to move. They then started to execute the badly injured. I was outside with many other less seriously hurt when we heard the firing and screaming. One person covered in blood jumped from a top floor window. We fled. Although UNITA started shooting at us, we managed to escape and make the road to Benguela.

UNITA's director of Huambo's hospital, Natanel Chimuco, admitted to Human Rights Watch that the greatest damage to his hospital was "in the crazy week after the siege." The hospital is now being renovated and, although it is short of drugs and equipment, it is treating civilians. Human Rights Watch found no soldiers in the hospital during its inspection, consistent with UNITA's claim that the hospital is used to treat civilians. Several known MPLA doctors remain treating civilian patients, although Human Rights Watch failed to gain free access to them.

The hospital was by no means the only building to suffer. Banks were robbed of all money, and shops and warehouses were looted of anything moveable. UNITA soldiers went around door-to-door searching for booty. Anyone who resisted risked being killed or beaten up. Very few people dared speak out about the "Semana de Locura" (Crazy Week) in Huambo. However, when Human Rights Watch was able to get away from the UNITA "guide" and interview in a confidential manner we obtained several accounts.

X is an Ovimbundu, born in Huambo, who voted for UNITA in the elections. He remained in Huambo with his family hoping that things would improve under UNITA control. This was not to be the case.

> They came looking for any suspected MPLA supporters and lists were drawn up. To prove their support people would tell names. Sometimes these names were not true but used to settle old grievances. Everybody had to prove their obedience to "*O Mais Velho*" [The Wise One, meaning Savimbi]. If we failed, we were under suspicion and could disappear. Hundreds did.

XX & XXX, relatives of mine, were executed in that week.
Also the city was looted. The government soldiers did not
have time to loot when they left. It was UNITA. Some of our
senior officials in Huambo gave orders in the purge and led
the looting. They should be made accountable. This was not
why I voted for Savimbi or according to his teachings. His
officials betray the faith we put in the party.

After the excesses of initial occupation, the situation in Huambo
stabilized. On June 1, 1993, the ICRC was able to evacuate the Portuguese
nationals who wished to leave on four aircraft. The city stands in ruins, partly
as a result of UNITA artillery and tank fire, but also from the frequent aerial
bombardment by government aircraft during and after the siege.

UNITA has since been focusing its attention on transforming Huambo
into its "capital." UNITA officials attempted to get Human Rights Watch to fill
out immigration forms on arrival at Huambo airport. Several UNITA officials
told Human Rights Watch in May 1994 that UNITA had found administrating
a large city such as Huambo a daunting task.

Neighborhood party groups (Direcçáo Política) control the different
sectors of the city. They pass serious problems and useful intelligence to
BRINDE, UNITA's security forces, on a regular basis. A police force is also
operational, distinguished by their arm bands. UNITA is trying to impose taxes
on remaining residents. Clinics are being set up across the city with some
success in an attempt to take drugs and medicines out of the black market so that
they can be properly prescribed. Huambo operates on a cash economy, using
Angolan currency even though the war has destroyed much of the local
economy.

Since January 1993 the population of Huambo city and its periphery (as
far as Caala) has shrunk from 750,000 to an estimated 400,000. About 220,000
people live in the city and 180,000 persons in the periphery extending about
fifteen miles from the center. Remaining urban residents have lost their incomes
and have been forced to sell their possessions. Population movements appear to
have been mostly to the west and northwest. There are reports of increasing
movements from the southeast of Angola into eastern and southeastern Huambo
province.[1]

---

[1] United Nations Humanitarian Assistance Coordination Unit (UCAH), "Briefing
Note: Overall Humanitarian Situation in Huambo," updated April 30, 1994.

Freedom of travel outside Huambo is still not permitted. *"Bilhetes"* are issued for passing through UNITA check points. These are required for travel between most municipalities, although there are a few exceptions. Huambo's markets were full of food, with traders going as far as Zambia and Namibia. Human Rights Watch also interviewed a trader who came from a government zone. In theory, this should not happen as both sides block freedom of movement across their front lines. But there seem to be plenty of exceptions as long as the right officials are paid off.

Underage Recruitment

Underage recruitment by UNITA is a serious problem in Huambo and elsewhere. In May Human Rights Watch witnessed a truck draw up at a market in central Huambo and soldiers grab young people. Some of these appeared to have been barely in their teens. Human Rights Watch was told in Huambo that the seized youth were often driven to the airport at night, put on planes and taken for training to locations nearer the military fronts. In May, an NGO in Huambo put up pictures of missing children outside its offices in an attempt to reunite families. UNITA took these down. The NGO then put them up inside, but these too were taken down. This suggests that UNITA may have seized the minors in question or its army. Human Rights Watch has recorded this disturbing and apparently growing pattern in other UNITA zones as well.

During March, April and May 1993, both the Angolan government and UNITA stifled efforts by humanitarian organizations to reach Huambo, and it was not until June 1993 that the ICRC, NGOs and the U.N. managed to fly in to assess the situation. Their initial assessments showed that Huambo's needs were concentrated mostly in the non-food sector, although salt, sugar, and vegetable oils were in very short supply. The humanitarian organizations were ready to establish relief programs, but the government bombed Huambo during August and September, making it impossible to reach the city. On October 18, the U.N. returned to Huambo, having brokered access to UNITA-occupied zones. Soon afterwards relief operations resumed and have continued more or less consistently since.

Kuito

The city of Kuito was devastated during a twenty-one-month siege by UNITA forces which began on January 5, 1993. From that date until September 1994, nobody was able to leave the city except foreign nationals. Those that crossed into UNITA zones were not heard from or seen again by the residents.

As in Huambo the majority of people in Kuito had voted for UNITA in the elections.

Human Rights Watch visited Kuito in May 1994 but was refused access to the UNITA sector of that city and Kunje by UNITA's Captain Pepe who manned the main checkpoint. He claimed that Brigadier Karinala Samy could authorize our visit, but was out of town. This was deliberate misinformation. We learned several hours later that Brig. Samy had been meeting the ICRC in Kuito at the very hour Capt. Pepe said he was out of town. It added to our suspicion that UNITA was preparing for further military action, and fighting resumed a day later.

It is believed that some 15,000 people died in 1993 in Kuito, either from the direct effects of war or indirectly through starvation or related diseases. In October 1994, Kuito's governor said at least 20,000 people had died in the siege from hunger, disease or wounds, but aid workers have put the figure above 30,000.[2]

When fighting started in January it was initially difficult to distinguish who was fighting whom in the fierce street battles around the city center. UNITA was driven out of Kuito on January 10, but within two days UNITA began a siege in earnest by shelling the city and shooting at any aircraft that tried to land at the airport. By April 1993, UNITA had been able to break the government's defenses and fight back to within a radius of some nine kilometers.

Subsequent fighting badly destroyed the city and UNITA took control of one area within it. By June the main avenue which led to and through the city had become the front line, marked out by lines of stones, waist- or shoulder-high walls of sandbags splitting and barricading divided streets, with antipersonnel mines and booby-trapped explosives in gutted backyards and buildings along the line.

Shelling

In July and August 1993, UNITA rained down some 1,000 heavy artillery shells on Kuito every day. Virtually every building in Kuito was damaged and UNITA had clearly made little attempt to target precisely its shelling. Casualty rates were high. On June 11, 1993, one shell killed thirty-nine people in central Kuito, wiping out several families. Shrapnel wounds are common. According to government military officials in Kuito, UNITA has used

---

[2] *Reuters*, October 11, 1994.

120mm artillery, 106mm recoilless rifles, and AGS 30mm rocket launchers during its siege.

The fighting had reduced the city's fine colonial buildings and pastel-painted villas to ruins. Not a single house emerged unscathed. Whole apartment blocks were gutted; their interiors spill onto the streets below. Many people had moved into the city center buildings to take refuge from UNITA's advances, with its artillery shells, mortars, and sniper fire. The inside of these buildings became blackened shells, housing thousands of refugees, mainly women and children, living side by side in squalid conditions, permanently covered in a thick gray smoke from cooking pots.[3]

From June 1993, UNITA inched its way forward, fighting block by block. By November, some 30,000 people, including non-combatants, soldiers and civilian militia, were trapped in an area of ten blocks. Between June 1993 and June 1994 the government held the eastern part of the city, containing most of the city center and some mud hut "bairro" neighborhoods. UNITA controlled the western and southeastern areas, including the central hospital.

As UNITA advanced toward the hospital in May, residents removed the medical supplies and equipment to the other side of town, but a UNITA shell hit the shop where it was kept. A ruined primary school was then turned into a hospital for the seriously wounded, while first aid posts sprung up across town. The one remaining Angolan doctor left the city in August 1993, crossing into UNITA zones. Paramedics and nurses continued meanwhile to try and treat victims without anesthetic and with rudimentary instruments. During the period June to October 1993, the local population survived by eating leaves, grass, banana roots and toasted maize. Thousands of children died and the adults lost between ten and twenty-five kilos on average. Current official estimates are that about 30,000 remain in the town on the government side. The population on the UNITA side has in contrast been able to take refuge in the outlying villages and soldiers are the only people from the UNITA side to be seen in the town. The previous population of the town was 150,000.

Church property was not exempt from the fighting either as it became a refuge for many from the fighting. As UNITA made gains, church buildings close to the changing front line were abandoned. On August 6 UNITA captured the bishopric building after fierce fighting and although UNITA tried to evacuate the bishop of Kuito, Pedro Luís António, he insisted that he and his staff stay, in an attempt to stop looting. However, government forces recaptured the

---

[3] See also Mercedes Sayagues, "The Siege of Cuito," *Africa Report*, January/February 1994.

bishopric on September 14. A tremendous battle ensued between UNITA and the government for control of the building over the next seven days with the bishop, his staff and refugees laying low inside the building. By September 21 UNITA recaptured the building and evacuated its residents to a military base near Kuito. Five days later they were transferred to Huambo. The bishopric was partially destroyed by the fighting, having been hit several times by grenades, 81mm and 122mm mortars and small arms fire.[4]

On September 21, 1993, a unilateral ceasefire was declared by UNITA which led to a fragile suspension of hostilities over the following weeks. A U.N. mission to Kuito was sent on October 12 to assess the situation and make contact with the local authorities on either side. As a result, the first U.N. World Food Program (WFP) cargo flight of humanitarian assistance was completed on October 16. However, the next day, the last of three scheduled WFP relief flights was not authorized to land by UNITA. This led to three WFP staff members being unable to leave Kuito. UNITA officials declared that they had not intended to detain the U.N. staff members but were concerned that operational modalities needed to be discussed before further cargo flights could be carried out. The WFP staff stayed in the city for three days until flights resumed on October 21. On October 29, the U.N. evacuated from Kuito to São Tome 121 non-Angolans (Portuguese and other foreigners) who had been trapped since the commencement of hostilities.

During the siege of the town, the government carried out airdrop operations targeting the population in government-held areas (Kuito and Kunje). When the U.N. started airlift operations, the government continued airdrop activities for civilians in Kunje and the military in Kuito. Incidents involving exchange of fire or disputes occur when parachutes of supplies fall on "no man's land" or UNITA territory. In November, recurring incidents of this nature resulted in heavy fighting between the government and UNITA forces in the area between Kunje and Kuito and around the town. All foreign personnel were evacuated on November 23 and humanitarian aid flights suspended. On

---

[4] Although both UNITA and government forces used the bishopric as a shield, neither side attempted to break in and use it as a military position during the fighting. However, UNITA snipers killed a woman as she knocked on the door of the bishopric in July, and on September 19, 1993 a sniper killed a Bulgarian teacher who had taken refuge in the building while he was briefly in view at dusk on its veranda. About twenty other civilians died in the bishopric during the January-September 1993 period from illness, starvation and war wounds. See also, António Moreira, "A Guerra Do Kuito-Bié," *Vida Consagrada*, No. 153, January 1994, pp. 18-28.

November 24, the situation was calmer and the WFP flights resumed. In December, things remained quiet, apart from an incident on December 11 when a WFP staff member in Kuito saw a government plane drop four bombs in UNITA areas close to the town.

On February 5, 1994 intense fighting broke out and continued throughout the week, killing hundreds of civilians and soldiers. The dispute originated over a tree branch in "no man's land" which government troops attempted to drag back to their side for firewood. Shots were initially fired into the air, but were aimed later at soldiers on the ground. A fire-fight ensued. The WFP was obliged to cancel relief flights and international NGO staff were evacuated by road to Huambo. Following negotiations by the U.N. with government and UNITA officials the WFP was able to fly again to Kuito on February 14 and the NGOs returned.[5]

The WFP was flying ninety tons of food each week to Kuito on average to provide 100,000 people, or 50,000 on each side, with a minimum diet. With probably some 30,000 living on the government side, these weekly shipments provided some cushion for residents, enabling them to survive when fighting halted the flights or when food was taken by soldiers. UNITA benefitted more. There were no civilians in its sector of the city; the civilians were forced to evacuate to the surrounding countryside. The food for UNITA was taken to a warehouse located a few miles from an important UNITA logistics base.

After lengthy negotiations UNITA also allowed U.N. and NGO officials to visit the government-held garrison town of Kunje on March 16 by road from Kuito. Kunje had been isolated from external contact for more than one year. The mission estimated that around 25-30,000 people were in need of assistance. Previously, the civilian population (mainly women) had been allowed by UNITA to come to Kuito on foot through well-known paths, but could only carry back two kilos of food.

On May 26, a day after Human Rights Watch left the city, fighting broke out again in Kuito, allegedly because drunken UNITA soldiers threw rocks and then grenades at a house in which a government military commander was holding a meeting. Hundreds of civilian casualties were reported. Nine days later, on June 4, international NGO workers were evacuated when a brief ceasefire was arranged. Two ICRC workers decided to stay but were evacuated eventually.

---

[5] United Nations Humanitarian Assistance Coordination Unit "Briefing Note: Overall Humanitarian Situation in Kuito," updated April 1994.

Kunje also was attacked by UNITA and heavily shelled. In this fighting the government, against expectations, succeeded in pushing UNITA out of the city, using air support. On June 2, government aircraft bombed UNITA positions including the Central Hospital. Aerial bombing of outlying UNITA positions continued on June 10 and 11. U.N. relief flights to Kuito resumed on September 12, but were halted by UNITA again three days later. Non-U.N. flights, by Africare and others, are being permitted.

Surprisingly, fraternization between UNITA and government soldiers was common during lulls in fighting. Human Rights Watch noted groups of UNITA and government soldiers mingling in the middle of the road along the front line. Government soldiers gambled salt or tins or sardines from government parachute drops for UNITA batches of firewood, a rarity in the city. Trade had become so regular that UNITA troops had set up makeshift breweries to produce "*cachipembe*," a strong maize-base liquor, for sale to government soldiers on the front line in barter deals. A trader told Human Rights Watch, "The soldiers control all trade. I get my produce from a commander. He takes most of the profit. He gets some things from UNITA. That is how it is."

Olegário Cardoso one of the most prominent businessmen who remain in the city, explained at his business premises, known as Casa Ford: "For a while the government decrees a ban on trade with UNITA, or UNITA issues orders to stop selling to the city, and the business stops. But it soon resumes because we need the firewood and they need salt and cloths. There are cousins and sometimes even brothers fighting each other across that line. This is a crazy war of crazy people. One minute they do business together and the next they kill each other."

Sniper Fire

Sniper fire in Kuito between June and September 1993 caused many casualties along government-held buildings facing the front line. To avoid snipers, people tore holes in walls, connecting all houses in each block, but still had to risk going out to get supplies and water. One particular sniper was very effective from his location on top of the cinema where he got a fine view of the front line. On one occasion a rope was thrown out from Casa Ford to an injured women to pull her in to safety before the sniper finished her off. Such testimonies are widespread in Kuito.

Alice, a twenty-four-year-old, lives across the road from Casa Ford at the ruined Hotel Kuito. She was an eyewitness to countless UNITA sniper shots.

Eleven people I know were killed by that UNITA sniper. He had a telescopic sight because it sometimes caught the sun. He shot old, young, women and children. Everybody was a potential target. He wanted to kill. Marcela, my sister, was shot in the leg by him. But he refused to stop. He shot her three times to ensure she was dead. We did not go out in daylight unless in an emergency and then only by running fast and not in straight lines. Moonlight was also really bad. But we needed fresh water. That UNITA can't be from around here. He would never try and kill his own people in that cold way.

Starvation of Civilians

Between April and September 1993 food security deteriorated rapidly in Kuito as government airdrops to the city were inaccurate and not substantial enough to feed the residents in the government-held sector. *"Batidas"* were formed in response to the growing scarcity of food and increasing malnutrition. These were large groups of desperate people who would cross the lines into UNITA territory to fetch food from the countryside. Sometimes two hundred strong, these groups braved heavy UNITA gunfire and minefields to find food. Casualty levels were sometimes as high as one-third of the party that set out. Hunger weakened the city's defenses. As the batidas became larger and had to venture out further, soldiers too abandoned their positions in search of food. Alcinda went with several of these batidas. She described what happened:

We were so hungry that we had to get out of the city and find food. We tried to do this silently as we already knew the paths. The danger was that UNITA had laid mines on these. In July [1993] I was with a group which entered into a newly laid UNITA minefield. Ten died and several injured crawled back. Soldiers came with us to help us find food and provide cover gunfire if UNITA saw us. Usually a batida ended up in gunfights as UNITA also kept a look-out for us, especially when we were heavily laden on our return. They could then collect and keep or sell to us what they had taken from our dead.

A nurse at the hospital confirmed that casualties were high during the "period of the batidas." She said, "We knew when a batida had taken place because the next day the injured would arrive. Sometimes they would reach us several days after the event, having only crept back at night because of UNITA snipers."

Divided families

There are countless cases of divided families in Kuito. Eduardo Sauro suffers badly from leprosy and his colony was taken over in early January by UNITA while he was in town looking for treatment. It is a few miles away behind UNITA lines and he waits for the day he can return home to join his wife and four children.

Vítor is a nine-year-old boy from Kunje. He was brought to Kuito for medical treatment and could not return when fighting started in January 1993. His mother, who had been with him, was killed in July by UNITA shelling. He does not know whether his father is still alive in the government-held town of Kunje, seven miles away.

Both are innocent victims of this war and depend for their survival on the relief work of international agencies when the government and UNITA rebels are willing to allow these to operate.

Because the cemetery remained on UNITA's side, the dead in Kuito are buried in gardens, parks, sidewalks, and front yards. They are also buried on balconies and rooftops by scattering whatever is available over them. Some of the mounds are marked with simple wooden crosses, others with bottles or branches of withered leaves.

Malanje

Human Rights Watch was unable to visit Malanje during its May-June 1994 Angola mission because flights were suspended due to long-range indiscriminate shelling by UNITA. These flights resumed on August 23.

In October 1992, the city came under siege by UNITA forces and it has remained so until the present day. At that time food reserves in the city were estimated as sufficient to last until May 1993 for the estimated population of 350-400,000, of which 310,000 are believed to have been displaced since the war resumed. Because of UNITA shelling and minefields, accessibility around the town has been, and still is, limited to some fifteen to twenty kilometers.

From June to August 1993, the situation in the city deteriorated sharply because of the lack of food supplies. U.N Special Representative Blondin Beye had declared in July that Malanje was too dangerous for U.N. planes to land, and continued to declare Malanje "out-of-bounds" in September, even though the situation was improved, with the Catholic relief agency Caritas flying aid in safely. In late September, the WFP started relief flights, ignoring Beye's orders. U.N. and foreign NGO officials told Human Rights Watch that Beye's refusal to permit massive airlifts to Malanje cost hundreds of lives.

In October 1993 the relief situation in Malanje had become so serious that there were frequent riots at the airport over arriving supplies. Many people were eating seeds provided to them for the planting season. In November 1993, Beye lifted his ban. By January 1994 the numbers of NGOs working in the city had increased from one to seven. By May 1994 eight World Food Program relief flights were landing in Malanje every day.[6] Although there has been a noticeable improvement in the conditions, the situation is still critical. People are still desperate to pick up any grain that has fallen from bags being unloaded at the airport or at the warehouses.

During December 1993 and January 1994 security again deteriorated. Staff members of CONCERN were injured and a World Vision International staff member was killed by security forces in two separate incidents. On January 5, 1994, mortar fire by UNITA on the airport prevented a plane carrying U.S. Congressmen from landing. A CONCERN feeding center, Cangambo-2, which the delegation was due to visit was also targeted. Several civilians were killed when an intoxicated police officer walked in and sprayed the building with AK-47 fire. Resumed UNITA shelling closed the airport on May 18, 1994. Without food flights, malnutrition rates soared and deaths from starvation began, with eighty-seven deaths reported in June and 113 in July 1994.

Landmines

Malanje suffers greatly from landmines. In desperate need of food, people daily risk their lives to go outside the city limits where the land is heavily mined in order to fetch cassava and firewood. The provincial authorities estimate that more than 20,000 women and 2,000 men leave the government-controlled area on an average of two to three times each week. In November 1993, at least five people a day were reportedly injured by mines, most of them while searching for food. In May 1994 the number had declined to five a week.

Because Malanje is surrounded by minefields that prevent farming, the city is almost totally dependent on airlifted food. Any suspension of relief flights forces people, especially women, to return to the cassava fields to rummage for food and firewood, although they know the fields are mined. Civilian mine

---

[6] United Nations Humanitarian Assistance Coordination Unit, "Briefing Note: Overall Humanitarian Situation in Malanje," updated January 9, 1994.

casualties become extremely high when relief flights are suspended, as demonstrated by the significant increase in the number of landmine incidents between May 18 and August 24, 1994, when flights were suspended.

UNITA has also infiltrated Malanje on sabotage missions. In early 1994 it placed antipersonnel mines outside doors, in an attempt to unnerve residents. There were several casualties.

STARVATION AS A METHOD OF COMBAT

UNITA has consistently used starvation of civilians as a method of combat, in violation of the rules of war. UNITA justifies this by claiming that the majority of the population in the besieged towns and cities are linked to the military. In cities like Malanje this is not the case. The majority are internally displaced who have fled their homes because of the war and do not want to live in UNITA zones. UNITA has made them captives in the towns they fled to by refusing to permit them unhindered safe passage to their chosen destination.

Even if the civilians are "linked to the military" because they are military dependents or relatives, or even if they are government supporters, that does not turn them into legitimate military targets. They remain civilians and are thus immune from attack.

Customary international law clearly prohibits the intentional starvation of civilians as a method of combat. Protocol II, Article 14,[7] places legal limits on the military tactic of targeting the civilian population by causing hunger, a prohibition from which no derogation may be made. No exception is for instance made for arguments of imperative military necessity. What is crucial is the intention of using starvation as a method or weapon to attack the civilian population.

Starvation of combatants, however, remains a permitted method of combat, as in siege warfare or blockades. A siege "consists of encircling an

---

[7] Protocol II, Article 14 - Protection of objects indispensable to the survival of the civilian population:
Starvation of civilians as a method of combat is prohibited. It is prohibited to attack, destroy, remove or render useless, for that purpose, objects indispensable to the survival of the civilian population, such as foodstuffs, agricultural areas for the production of foodstuffs, crops, livestock, drinking water installations and supplies and irrigation works.

enemy location, cutting off those inside from any communication in order to bring about their surrender."[8] This is theoretically aimed at preventing military material from reaching combatants. But, except in the case of food supplies being specifically intended as provisions for combatants, it is prohibited to destroy or attack objects indispensable for civilian survival, even if the adversary may benefit from them.[9] Even if the army might be diverting civilian relief food, selling it or illegally benefiting from it—which is what has happened across Angola and which is also a violation of the rules of war—relief destined for civilians should not therefore be blocked, confiscated, prevented or destroyed. Furthermore, under the duty to distinguish civilians from combatants, the besieging forces may not close their eyes to the effect upon civilians of a food blockade or siege. It is well recognized that, "in case of shortages occasioned by armed conflict, the highest priority of available sustenance materials is assigned to combatants".[10]

A commentary by the International Committee of the Red Cross notes that: "Starvation can also result from an omission. To deliberately decide not to take measures to supply the population with objects indispensable for its survival in a way would become a method of combat by default, and would be prohibited under this rule."[11]

UNITA's military actions since January 1993 against humanitarian relief operations are well documented. UNITA's tactics range from direct shooting at aircraft to shelling airstrips in order to close them. UNITA has also been responsible for planting new antipersonnel mines on paths and in fields around Kuito and Malanje to make rummaging for food by the residents more difficult, in turn causing more hardship for them. The fact that the government also bombs airstrips to stop humanitarian aid from reaching UNITA-controlled zones does not justify UNITA's attempts to starve the civilian population.

Some examples of UNITA attacks of this kind in 1993 and 1994 follow:

●   July 14, 1994: UNITA shot at a World Food Program plane as it approached to land at Malanje. The relief flight had received the standard

---

[8] ICRC, *Commentary on the Additional Protocols*, p.1457.

[9] See Chapter Eight.

[10] Bothe, *New Rules for Victims of Armed Conflicts*, p.680.

[11] ICRC, *Commentary on the Additional Protocols*, p.1458.

clearance from both the government and UNITA. Relief flights were subsequently suspended.

• June 21, 1994: UNITA attacked a relief convoy with mortar and small arms fire, destroying fifteen WFP vehicles between Lobito and Bocoio. Two WFP workers were wounded.

• June 10, 1994: UNITA shelled a clearly marked WFP plane at Balombo (Benguela) while it was unloading. The flight had been authorized by both sides.

• May 31, 1994: UNITA shelled Malanje airport after U.N. light aircraft landed to evacuate international relief workers, putting their lives at risk. The U.N. flights had been authorized by both sides.

• May 27, 1994: UNITA began shelling Malanje airport just as an authorized WFP aircraft was trying to land. The plane aborted its landing.

• May 20, 1994: WFP suspended relief flights to Malanje after UNITA fired seven shots at a WFP plane as it was preparing to land at the airport. The flight had been authorized by both sides.

• April 19, 1994: UNITA shelled Malanje airport while a WFP plane was unloading its cargo. The flight had authorization.

• March 3, 1994: WFP suspended flights to Malanje after UNITA shelled the airport during take-off of a WFP plane. The flight had been authorized by both sides.

• August 26, 1993: UNITA soldiers attacked three trucks that left a WFP relief convoy of seventy-five vehicles and killed three truckers. A policeman was subsequently killed as he examined the booby-trapped corpse of one of the truckers. One vehicle was destroyed and two were partially damaged.

• July 15, 1993: UNITA soldiers fired bullets at a U.N. relief aircraft as it tried to land at M'banza Congo (then under UNITA control).

• April 26, 1993: UNITA shot down a U.N. relief plane with a missile at 16,000 feet, thirty kilometers outside of Luena. The plane crash-landed in a minefield and the plane's Russian engineer was killed by a mine he stepped on after leaving the plane. The remaining seven crew members were injured.

• April 5, 1993: U.N. relief aircraft flying to Uíge and M'banza Congo (UNITA-controlled) were fired at by UNITA upon arrival.

HUMANITARIAN ASSISTANCE

The number of Angolans affected by the civil war has been estimated by the U.N. Humanitarian Assistance Coordination Unit (UCAH) at 3.3 million, including 2,110,000 persons directly affected by the conflict, 950,300 internally displaced persons (deslocados), 112,000 drought-affected, and 112,000 returnees. The majority of these people increasingly depend on relief aid for their survival. Although the politics of opening up zones for relief distribution has been delicate and often slow, the international relief effort has successfully put mass starvation on hold.

In May 1993 fighting intensified in some parts of the densely populated provinces of Huambo, Bié and Benguela. Humanitarian conditions deteriorated daily as relief operations had to be suspended. In an attempt to counter this, the U.N. presented a one-month Emergency Relief Plan (ERP) to the two sides in May 1993. It proposed establishing four roads and ten air corridors for humanitarian assistance. Agreement on this was finally reached on June 21, 1993. WFP flights were successful in reaching Huambo, Luena and Saurimo, but the operation was subsequently suspended because of intense fighting in Kuito and UNITA's unwillingness to open windows of access to the town. In July both sides approved a modified emergency plan to deliver relief flight supplies to fifteen locations, eight of them in UNITA-controlled areas. On July 15, the U.N. flights restarted. But, after two flights to Luena and Mavinga/Jamba, a WFP plane was fired upon by UNITA as it was preparing to land in M'Banza Congo. At the same time UNITA prevented a scheduled flight from arriving at Kuito for security reasons. Once again relief flights to the besieged cities were suspended.

The suspension prompted civilians to move westward to the overcrowded government-controlled urban areas along the coast. WFP and Caritas started airlift operations to Cabinda, Saurimo, Luena and Dundo using chartered aircraft. In mid-August Uíge was added to the list. Land corridors such as Luanda to Dondo and Sumbe, and Lubango to various destinations were also maintained.

Faced with an increasingly complex situation, the U.N. defined three categories of relief operations: no-conflict areas (coastal strip), non-intensive conflict areas, and intensive conflict areas. The objective was to start airlifting to nine destinations, four of them to active conflict areas (Huambo, Kuito, Malanje and Menongue). The government approved the U.N. plan in late July 1993 and UNITA did so on September 3 after a special meeting with U.N. representatives in Kinshasa. Soon after, on September 21, UNITA declared its unilateral cessation of hostilities throughout the country and the level of conflict gradually declined until late December. In mid-October the U.N. finally gained access to Kuito and a few days later relief flights began to Huambo. In November and December the emergency relief program rapidly expanded, but in February 1994 fierce fighting resumed in Kuito and the subsequent heavy shelling of Malanje caused a suspension of relief flights to both cities for nearly a week. Flights resumed on February 18 following negotiations. Relief flights to Malanje were again suspended on May 21 following shelling. The government then imposed a temporary ban on flights to Huambo, Jamba and Uíge, a ban which was soon extended to flights to all conflict zones following continued heavy UNITA shelling of Malanje and Kuito and government bombing of Huambo. Flights were able to resume to all destinations except Kuito and Malanje in mid-July.[12]

UNITA OUTSIDE THE MAIN TOWNS

A current Human Rights Watch researcher was in Malanje province at the time of the Angolan elections, and witnessed the mobilization of armed UNITA soldiers in Massango municipality on the election days. UNAVEM officials in Quela saw UNITA soldiers uncover caches of weapons on September 28, the day before the elections. On October 3, following an inflammatory radio broadcast by Jonas Savimbi, mobilization began to accelerate across the municipalities. In Cacuso, following the broadcast, local people saw UNITA soldiers uncovering hidden weapons caches. Some in the local population began digging pits to hide their precious belongings. Many civilians had decided that renewed conflict would result and began their preparations for it. It was a well-rehearsed routine of a people with decades of experience of living in conflict zones.

Soon after the elections UNITA began to capture municipalities across the country. Richard Fritz, the U.S. Defense Attache in Luanda at the time, described UNITA's offensive as "Pac-Manning [after the video game] their way through the municipalities. When their score got too high, the government struck back." Civilians caught in outlying towns and municipalities during UNITA's offensive suffered great hardship and many encountered human rights abuses.

Summary Executions
Among the accounts given to Human Rights Watch was that of Seloka, a 16-year-old married woman who arrived in Zambia in 1993, having fled the war from Ninda (Moxico). She described the situation she saw during the 1992

---

[12] United Nations Humanitarian Assistance Coordination Unit, "Briefing on Progress of Humanitarian Assistance in Angola 1993-4."

election period when UNITA was preparing to take full control of the municipalities.

> I left because of war. I have seen this. My brothers, Mulenga and Mossole, were killed by UNITA a few days before the elections. They were taken into the bush and axed. I saw the bodies, but was not allowed to bury them. Afterwards UNITA told us that we would have to transport weapons for them and they would be back in a few days. I and some other relatives then decided to flee the area.

Another was that of 56-year-old Francisco, a father of seven children. He described how UNITA attacked his village Namalatala (Nambuangongo municipality, Bengo province) without warning on April 12, 1993.

> UNITA suddenly attacked us and killed two people they said were known to them as MPLA spies. They were shot and cut into pieces. We were not allowed to bury them and UNITA said it was coming back to take us the next day to a new area for our safety. They gave no warning before their attack. We decided at a village meeting to flee and it took us three months of walking to reach safety at Boa Esperança. We lived in the bush hiding from the soldiers, sometimes for days, until it seemed safe to move on. Life is terrible now. We used to eat well in the village. Now we are hungry and live without pride.

Forced Portering

Forced portering also took place. Luísa, no stranger to life in UNITA zones, arrived in Zambia in 1993 having had enough of war.

> I fled from Lumbala Nguimbo (Moxico) because of the war. UNITA is causing the problem, forcing people to fight, and taking food from them when they cannot already easily live. During the elections I voted [showed her card]. Then UNITA began killing people it believed had supported the MPLA, after it lost the elections. All Lumbala residents were at risk because the town voted MPLA. Before the elections UNITA had warned people to vote for it, but we wanted to express our right. They either kill or put you in pit prisons if you don't

obey them. My father, Ngubu, was killed in 1993 by UNITA when he consistently refused to carry weapons and ammunition for UNITA. He was killed in the Lumbala triangle.

I know UNITA. I have been used as a porter to carry weapons and ammunition for UNITA for many years. I never travelled by vehicle. But I travelled far, to Lungebungu, even Huambo. The weight of what I carried was too heavy, never light. Some walks took a month, others two. Usually ten civilians go, with six soldiers to escort them.

The soldiers looked after themselves and I was never abused by them. However, if a porter slowed down or collapsed the soldiers would wait but would become angry. Sometimes they beat us. Nobody else could carry the loads. Many people tried to run away.

"Taxation" of Food

All the accounts of those interviewed suggested that hunger remains a severe problem in these southern and eastern UNITA zones. International relief aid does not appear to be reaching the needy civilians in any quantity. "Taxation" of food by soldiers is high and freedom of movement is tightly controlled. Mungo and his family of five arrived in Zambia from Jamba in April 1994. They described the situation in Jamba as very difficult for civilians. Mungo said:

There is starvation and no medicine or assistance for us although there has been no fighting around Jamba. It is forbidden to leave Jamba. All young men are conscripted into the UNITA army. There are still soldiers and military trained at Jamba. The soldiers grab the food we have, as they are also hungry. We had to escape. What the WFP brings feeds the soldiers and if they are still hungry we must go into the fields to find food for them.

Mistreatment of Government Soldiers

Some of the refugees in Zambia were former government soldiers who had been stuck in UNITA zones. Domingos F. came to Zambia in December 1993. A well-educated government soldier, he left Angola because of "suffering. There was not even salt."

> I was based at Lumbala N'guimbo (Moxico). During the election the MPLA brought clothing, food and salt for the residents. But UNITA grabs and kills. Straight after the elections they took over the town and put us in prison. My mother was killed by UNITA. Us soldiers had nowhere to flee and we were put behind bars. Many of my colleagues died. We were given no medical assistance and little food or water. Finally in mid-1993 I was released and used for portering duties, taking military equipment to the fronts. I escaped on one of these caravans.

Wanton Brutality

Mikakanga is a middle-aged woman who has no idea of her exact age. She arrived in Zambia in June 1993. She has lived in UNITA zones since 1982. She witnessed extreme brutality by UNITA soldiers following the elections:

> I am from Kangombe (Moxico) and ran away from war to Zambia. UNITA was killing people. Because of Savimbi we could not travel and we became hungry. Many people have been killed in Kangombe. The Savimbi tie people to trees, remove their clothing and cut them up with axes. All the time there is killing. My father and mother were killed by Savimbi. I saw their bodies. Few are lucky. They kill because the town voted MPLA. They do not choose, they kill. They grab you when you are in the fields.
>
> I fled when the Savimbi came asking for sons. I told them that I had none so they beat me. I then fled. Since the elections there have been new problems, great hunger, no clothing, not even salt. They also come asking for daughters, wanting them to carry weapons or marry them. If you refuse, they kill.

A very old woman called Tumba fled in 1993. She too had suffered much, as she told Human Rights Watch:

> I fled because of the war. People are dying. I come from a
> village called Kowa (near Kangombe). Savimbi is the trouble.
> Any young man is grabbed to fight. They took my grandson
> Makai. All the people are suffering the same. If you go
> farming they can assassinate you. What you have, the soldiers
> take. Savimbi has been in control for many years but it is now
> too bad to live there. When Makai was taken we decided to
> leave and ran away with my Uncle Caverla. The Savimbi head
> in our area was Kangangeni and his deputy, Mose, a resident
> of the area. They tell you to transport weapons. If you go
> wrong, they kill you. If you refuse after they have asked you
> two or three times, they kill you.

Former staunch UNITA supporters have also been leaving UNITA zones because of the extreme burden put on them. Mr. Jamba, a young man in his early thirties, arrived recently from Jamba in May 1994. He had joined his extended family which had been in the camp longer. One of his brothers there was an MPLA supporter; the family was divided by politics. Jamba said:

> Savimbi has been OK to me for twenty-two years. But the
> leaders have now changed their system. There is no longer
> food or money, while the leaders still are getting fat. Those
> days they used to have food. Now because of drought, people
> have no food. They are also not allowed to leave. We have to
> escape. The soldiers now take priority for all food. There is
> not enough for us. In the old days, a plane, 'Palma, used to
> arrive every two or three weeks to Jamba with supplies. Now
> it has stopped. During the elections the U.N. people were
> calming the situation between the MPLA and UNITA. The
> U.N. was biased against UNITA. The war is a result of
> internal callousness. MPLA is killing people with silencer
> guns, even during the ceasefire period. Some people who left
> Jamba to vote in the elections were killed by MPLA. João
> Vanafu, Mário N'gambu in Luena, for example.

Caminga, a 29-year-old man, arrived in Zambia from Jamba on January 6, 1994. He had worked as a telephone operator at UNITA's former headquarters and tells a similar story of growing hunger:

> I left because of hunger and because conditions have deteriorated in Jamba. The soldiers are also hungry and are causing greater problems for us civilians. Food comes from Namibia, especially Rundu in 1991 and 1992. It was either trucked in or brought on foot by porters. Oil was also sometimes brought in. Other times it has been flown in from Huambo or South Africa. However it is always insufficient. The time of Savimbi was a time of plenty. It is no longer, because Savimbi does not stay in Jamba. We also have problems of medical care. Juniors only have access to basic care—they are given aspirins. The big ones get what they need. Medicine is hidden for them.

In one of the most despicable incidents in recent years, UNITA forces attacked a train carrying civilians between Quipungo and Matala on May 27, 1993, resulting in the death of 225 persons, including women and children, and several hundred wounded. The appalling attack drew a rebuke from the U.N. Security Council:

> The Security Council strongly condemns this action by UNITA, which is a clear violation of Security Council resolutions and of international humanitarian law.... The Security Council expresses its condemnation of such criminal attacks and it stresses that those responsible must be held accountable.[13]

UNITA admitted carrying out the attack, but claimed that the train was transporting military personnel and supplies.

---

[13] Statement by the President of the Security Council, 3232nd meeting, June 8, 1993, in United Nations Department of Public Information, Reference Paper, "The United Nations and the Situation in Angola, May 1991-June 1994," (undated).

UNDERAGE RECRUITMENT

Under the rules of war, recruitment, voluntary or involuntary, of soldiers under the age of fifteen is illegal. Under the Convention on the Rights of the Child, those who recruit soldiers between the ages of fifteen and eighteen must endeavor to give priority to those who are the oldest. Although it is not yet in effect, the African Convention on the Rights of the Child prohibits recruitment of anyone under the age of eighteen. Human Rights Watch opposes recruitment of anyone under the age of eighteen. (See Chapter Eight).

UNITA's Governor of Huambo, Jerónimo Elavoko Wanga, told Human Rights Watch during a meeting in Huambo in May that UNITA's conscription age is twenty, but that eighteen-year-olds can volunteer. However, it is clear that involuntary recruitment of children and teenagers by UNITA is widespread and increasing.

José, a 19-year-old, arrived in Zambia from Luena on December 18, 1993. UNITA surrounded the town in January and began grabbing young men.

> I was taken to Lumbala and then Cunja. I was imprisoned and told I would go to Jamba for military training. Local people told me that I would be killed in Jamba. So I ran away. I was with a large group that UNITA had captured. We were too many for them to control, so some escaped and went home. My group was taken to Cunje, where they were left to recover. We then escaped. We have heard nothing about an earlier group that left to Jamba. We escaped because we eat at 1600 hours, the soldiers eat later. That evening it rained so soldiers sheltered under some trees. Six of us ran away, a seventh stayed.

José said that UNITA made no attempt to check their ages on capture, but that their ages ranged from eleven to twenty-eight.

SLAVE-LIKE CONDITIONS

A group of eight young people arrived in Zambia from Luena on August 30, 1993. Their names and ages were Tome (19); Tito (14); António

(17); Joaquim (18); Kalembe (17); Augusto (13); Vítor (18) and Ghadaffi (28). Tito told the story:

> We lived on the outskirts of Luena and UNITA found us in our homes on June 6, 1993. They then used us to carry weapons and food supplies. We became hungry and were not given any new clothing. All we had to eat was Nysima. At Rumbala we were told we would be given military training at Jamba so we could fight the MPLA. Brigadier Vicente of UNITA told us this. He is the UNITA commander for the region and has the reputation for organizing the war in the area. Local people warned us to try and escape because we would be killed at Jamba.
>
> We were marched with rope tied to each of our necks like a slave yoke and were forced to walk long distances each day. At night the yoke was untied. One day when we woke up and went to collect firewood we decided to escape. We ran away.

Some new arrivals have escaped from over a decade of suffering in UNITA zones. João is a 39-year-old teacher from Lumbala, who arrived in 1993. He, too, has noticed a change since the elections:

> The war since the elections has been different. There is now great hunger, no clothes, not even salt. UNITA is also now capturing children, they come and pick them up. Two younger brothers of mine have been taken by them.
>
> I have lived with UNITA for a long time. In 1986 they put me in an eight-meter pit prison in Mavinga. There was no sanitation and they fed me like a pig with a spoonful of cooked maize per day. I was imprisoned because I was a teacher. They believed that I was trying to escape and had been communicating with the MPLA. I had been reported by UNITA spies in the town. The spies were former UNITA soldiers from the 1960s who lived among us.
>
> I was released from prison when they remembered I was a teacher and were short of teachers. I was made to teach in

Mavinga without pay. In 1988 I sought permission to move back to Lumbala because my wife had become ill and was going blind. I used a Head Man to talk to Vicente who gave permission. From 1988 to 1991 I was made teacher at Muachavu base [a three-hour walk from his home]. All the "young stars" [new recruits] were at this base, brought here when captured for training. The base had few health facilities. We were given Chloroquine in water for every illness.

In 1991 to 1993 I was moved to teach at Metete for the UNITA administration. I was near the border and wondered if life might be better in Zambia. In 1992 I returned to Lumbala to vote in the elections. In early 1993 I escaped. After the elections big problems started. So I ran away. Many others have tried, many fail. Others stay because their relatives are too old or sick to move. Any problem with UNITA can land you in the pit or in prison. Suffering became too much after the elections.

Maria has also lived in UNITA zones since 1982. She arrived in April 1993 from Ninda (Moxico).

UNITA forced us to carry weapons. If we refused we would be beaten or arrested. The UNITA police lived in a camp in center of town. They were well known. I was once kicked by them like a football when they thought I might try and escape.

UNITA digs big holes in the bush and puts people in them who refuse to work for them. They kill people too. Soldiers take everything from us. Eventually I decided to run away to Mungu (Zambia) with my uncle after the elections, as things got bad. Commandante Nola is the senior UNITA commander in this area. But the real power is Vicente Viemba, No. 1. He obtains his orders direct from Savimbi. Anastácio is No. 2 and Sangumba is No. 3. Vicente gives out orders, but never carries these out himself. In our area the chiefs and headmen have lost their power to the military. The military determine what happens. UNITA has its own witchcraft. Their healers live a privileged life compared with us and they give the soldiers powers through their potions.

My family was ordered to build Vicente's house for him [without pay]. It is in the middle of the camp surrounded by soldiers. They are located in different positions according to their rank and department. Vicente's house had four rooms, made of wood, grass, and mud. UNITA has its politicians and party but the military is the power of Savimbi. They are the ones that live in comfort.

SOBAS

António Quisapa is a 74-year-old *soba* (traditional chief) who was caught in Kuito when the war broke out. He has been unable to return to his people and has been surviving on government hand-outs. He told Human Rights Watch that both sides have their sobas. In his village UNITA had appointed its own soba. He said, "No one respects traditional power any more, they just use us for their own ends."

In May 1994, Human Rights Watch witnessed a delegation of sobas being fed at the Hotel Cruz (UNITA's Party hotel) in Huambo, while they waited for an audience with Savimbi. They had already been waiting ten days and were getting frustrated. In a free moment one of the sobas told Human Rights Watch, "They show no respect for us. They keep us as waiting as pets. What can we do? To not assist is more dangerous, so we wait." But other UNITA officials argue that the sobas do have power and can curtail abuses of power by UNITA officials by reporting them to the senior leadership during these meetings.

PRISONERS

UNITA holds large numbers of government prisoners. It has provided the ICRC some access to these prisoners; in 1993 the ICRC visited a UNITA camp in Uíge holding 287 prisoners and in May 1994 the ICRC for the first time visited government prisoners held by UNITA in Huambo. While in Huambo Human Rights Watch established that these prisoners were being held there as an interim measure before being sent to "reeducation camps." Human

Rights Watch was told that at the reeducation camps captured soldiers were prepared to work for UNITA as porters, and rewarded with better conditions if they joined UNITA as soldiers. Their new loyalty was often tested by being sent on missions against government forces.

HOSTAGES

Common Article 3 (1) of the Geneva Conventions forbids the taking of hostages. (See Chapter Eight). UNITA has had a history of taking foreigners hostage in the past. Following the elections in 1992 and again in 1993 UNITA continued to take and attempt to take hostages.

During the October-November 1992 battle for Luanda, UNITA took hostage the Zimbabwean Ambassador, two Bulgarian embassy employees, and a British couple, David and Eleonore Chambers. They were used as human shields in an attempt by UNITA leaders, including Vice President Jeremias Chitunda and Elias Salupeto Pena, to escape from Miramar during the siege.[14] UNITA also broke into the U.S. Embassy compound in Miramar twice during the fighting in search of hostages, but failed to find the staff. The U.S. took the threat of UNITA abduction of its staff so seriously that a U.S. hostage-rescue unit was rushed to Brazzaville, Congo to be on stand-by.

David Chambers has described his and his wife's abduction and miraculous escape to Human Rights Watch. UNITA soldiers took Mr. and Mrs. Chambers at gunpoint from the Swedish Ambassador's residence. They were held, along with two employees of the Bulgarian Embassy, under armed guard for twenty-four hours in a darkened room, during which time they were fed once.

The leaders tried to escape in the first convoy of three cars. Chitunda[15] and Salupeto Pena were in the leading Mercedes,

---

[14]   An excerpt from Chitunda's diary, which Human Rights Watch has seen, demonstrates that the hostages were viewed as human shields: "And already there is an American woman among the Bulgarians and Zimbabweans who were taken from their diplomatic residences to Miramar—in the hope that if foreign diplomats are here, QTT [the MPLA] would hesitate to bomb and let us die with them."

[15]   Human Rights Watch has been told by other sources that Chitunda was in a different convoy that left an hour later. He was killed in his attempt to leave the city.

we followed in a Toyota Camry with four UNITA troopers, the third car was full of armed troopers. The convoy travelled at 100 miles per hour through Angolan government-held territory and was under fire from all sides for about 2.5 kilometers.

All [other] occupants of our car were killed by the gunfire and the car crashed at approximately 80 miles per hour when the driver was shot, somersaulting some six or seven times and coming to rest on the roof. We believe that all sixteen members of our convoy were killed, including Salupeto Pena and Chitunda.

We were under no doubts that we were hostages. Just before we left the UNITA quarters we were given access to a phone to contact our embassy to advise them of our predicament and ask for them to intervene with the Angolan government to prevent an attack on the UNITA premises.

Our escape from death was miraculous, both from the government gunfire and the eventual car crash. We continued to be under threat from the government forces who believed that we were part of UNITA.

In November 1993 UNITA took hostage twenty Brazilian and fifty Russian construction workers at the Capanda dam project (Malanje), as well as seven Britons and some 400 other expatriates (Portuguese, Filipinos, Brazilians and South Africans) at the diamond town of Cafunfo (Lunda Norte). There was little bloodshed in Cafunfo as outnumbered government troops stayed in the barracks. All the expatriate captives were kept under house or hostel arrest and were guarded by armed UNITA soldiers. They were eventually released. A diamond industry source told Human Rights Watch that most of the foreigners were well treated, although several who had tried to save some "assets" from falling into UNITA's hands were badly beaten up.

After the oil installations at Soyo fell for the first time to UNITA on January 19, 1993, UNITA held twenty expatriate hostages (fourteen Portuguese, two Indonesians, one Argentine, three Britons) for three weeks before transporting them to Uíge to be flown to Brazzaville, the Congolese capital, and freedom. One of the three British oil workers was injured when a government bomber attacked Uíge as they were about to leave.

Foreign nationals in besieged towns and cities were less lucky. Some, such as Portuguese nationals in Huambo, were held for over a month after the city fell to UNITA before the ICRC was permitted to fly them out. In the besieged city of Kuito, Portuguese nationals were only evacuated after nine months of fighting.

On August 26, 1994, UNITA soldiers at a roadblock north of Porto Amboim (Cuanza Sul) stopped a Toyota displaying an Africare logo and abducted its passengers: two Africare employees (Angolan Oliveira Cafranca Lembe and Congolese Vicente D. Douma), a Portuguese priest, and two or three nuns. They are still being held. This is only the second time in twenty-three years in Africa that Africare has had workers taken hostage.[16]

INDISCRIMINATE LAYING OF MINES

Mine warfare has intensified since hostilities resumed in October 1992, with thousands of new mines being used to obstruct roads and bridges, to encircle besieged towns with mine belts up to three kilometers wide and to despoil agricultural lands in combat zones.

The U.N. estimates that there are some nine to fifteen million mines laid throughout the country. Their legacy has had a devastating effect on Angolan society. The U.N. estimates that the number of mine amputees will reach 70,000 in 1994.[17] Mines have killed many thousands more, while impeding the delivery of humanitarian assistance and interfering with vital agricultural production.[18]

Human Rights Watch's investigations into weapons flows into Angola from 1993 onwards suggest that new purchasing of landmines has been a low priority to both sides. The implication is that both sides had maintained

---

[16] Interview with Africare in Washington, D.C., October 12, 1994.

[17] U.N. Department of Humanitarian Affairs, "1994 United Nations Revised Consolidated Inter-Agency Appeal for Angola, February-July 1994," p. 39.

[18] A U.S. official in November 1993 estimated the landmine toll at 16,000 dead and 40,000 maimed. James Woods in "The Quest for Peace in Angola," Hearing before the House Foreign Affairs Subcommittee on Africa, November 16, 1993, pp. 9-10.

sufficient stockpiles to resume mine warfare without hindrance in 1993-94. If the conflict is protracted, new purchases can be expected as old stocks run out.

In its January 1993 survey of landmines in Angola, Human Rights Watch identified thirty-seven types of mine deployed in Angola.[19] These originated from countries such as Belgium, former Czechoslovakia, China, France, former West Germany, Italy, former Soviet Union, United Kingdom, United States and former Yugoslavia.

Since the elections, there has been no significant change in the way mines are used by both armies, though there does appear to be a less random dissemination of them in and around villages except near the front lines. As front lines shift, the use of mines and the contamination of new areas increases.

In the interim period before the elections, some mined areas on the Planalto had been cleared. For the most part, these areas have remained free of mines, because UNITA occupied the areas so quickly after the elections that there was no need for mine warfare. Humanitarian agencies have been surprised at the extent to which roads in some UNITA-controlled zones are currently clear of mines, and are using these roads in their relief operations.

Nevertheless mines continue to take a tremendous toll on civilians, ensuring that Angola continues to have one of the highest per capita rates of landmine victims in the world.

Human Rights Watch interviewed twenty recent mine victims from Caxito, Malanje, Menongue (Cuando Cubango), Huambo, and Kuito. The majority were civilians who had not been given any warning about the presence of mines. In the cases of residents of besieged towns, they were often aware of the mines, but were starving and risked entering mined zones to collect food and firewood for cooking.

Children continue to be under a special risk from mines, as simple innocent playing can be very dangerous for them. J.M., a seven-year-old, was playing in Huambo's San Antonio suburb in April 1994 when he saw what seemed to be a tin can and kicked it. It exploded and ripped apart his left leg so that it had to be amputated at the knee. It was apparently a remotely delivered, "scatterable" mine, of which the government had dropped large numbers by air in order to protect the flank of its retreating troops in March 1993. J.M. was still in the Central Hospital when Human Rights Watch saw him, and he is worried that he will never be able to play football again.

---

[19] Africa Watch, *Landmines in Angola.*

Walking along a river can also result in tragedy. L.V., a twelve-year-old from Caxito, was walking along the banks of the Rio Dande on a fishing trip when he stepped on a mine. He was evacuated to Luanda where his right leg was amputated.

Searching for food around besieged cities and towns is extremely dangerous. In Kuito and Malanje women regard mines as an occupational hazard. They have to risk the mines or starve. This was the case for M.C., a thirty-seven-year-old mother of six, three of whom were killed by UNITA shelling in June 1993. She had survived the worst of UNITA's siege of Kuito, but in February 1994, when she went to look for wood in the "no-man's-land" surrounding the city, she stepped on a mine on a small path she had used previously many times. The mine shredded her right leg and she took twelve hours to crawl along the path back into Kuito and seek medical treatment. She blames UNITA for the mine, but regards herself as lucky to be alive. She knew twenty other women who had been injured by mines, and most of them died of their injuries in the fields.

A.H. is twenty-three and the mother of three. She was searching for cassava outside Malanje with a group of other women when she stepped on a mine in October 1993. Three others in the group also stepped on mines on the same trip. A.H. was carried back to Malanje and her right leg was amputated at the knee. She was able to find a space on a government flight out of the city and now lives in Luanda with relatives.

S.T. is a 17-year-old conscript soldier from Luanda. He was looking for food outside the town of Menongue in May 1994. While walking along a path to the fields, he tripped a wire that he did not see. The tripwire mine exploded and injured his left leg. He was evacuated by the military to Luanda and was treated at Luanda's Josina Machel hospital following amputation of the leg.

The seriousness of the mine problem has prompted UCAH to plan for the establishment of a Central Mine Action Unit which will be responsible for planning and coordinating mine clearance and mine awareness activities, as well as assisting in raising funds.[20] A consultant, Guy Lucas, has been employed to set up the unit. He has been travelling around Angola on an assessment mission in both government and UNITA zones. To date, the government has given him wider access than has UNITA. Currently, the German-based organization Cap Anamur is conducting demining in the south, and claims to have cleared 76,000

---

[20] Department of Humanitarian Affairs, "1994 United Nations Revised Consolidated Inter-Agency Appeal for Angola," February-July 1994, p.39.

mines in Angola. In addition, the U.K.-based Mines Advisory Group has a project in Luena. The World Food Program has signed a letter of intent with Swedrelief and the government's Instituto Nacional de Estradas de Angola (INEA) for a joint demining project to be implemented after the signing of a peace agreement. It would focus on the Luanda-Malanje and Benguela-Huambo-Kuito road corridors.

Customary international law and the 1980 Landmines Protocol govern the use of landmines. Human Rights Watch believes that landmines are an indiscriminate weapon, and that the use of landmines should be prohibited altogether under the requirements of customary international law. It is evident that the great majority of landmines in Angola have been deployed in flagrant disregard of the provision of the Landmines Protocol. Human Rights Watch concludes that only a complete global ban on the production, stockpiling, trade, and use of antipersonnel landmines can alleviate the human suffering caused by these weapons.[21]

---

[21] See, Human Rights Watch and Physicians for Human Rights, *Landmines: A Deadly Legacy* (New York: Human Rights Watch, 1993) for a comprehensive assessment of the global landmines crisis.

VII. THE U.N. AND INTERNATIONAL MEDIATION ATTEMPTS[1]

AFTER THE ELECTIONS

Since the September 29-30, 1992, presidential and legislative elections, the U.N. has actively tried to mediate in the conflict.[2] On October 7, four commissions of inquiry were established to investigate UNITA's claims of election fraud. The commissions consisted of officials from the U.N., UNITA, the MPLA, the CNE, and the Troika governments. The former U.N. Special Representative Margaret Anstee played a central role on October 10 in pressuring both sides to agree to an investigation into allegations of electoral fraud following the October 5 withdrawal in protest by UNITA of its forces from the new FAA army. The U.N. Security Council ad hoc Commission to Angola, composed of representatives of Cape Verde, Morocco, the Russian Federation and the United States who visited Angola between October 11 and 14, was mandated to meet key political, military and diplomatic figures and to attempt to generate support for the full implementation of the Bicesse agreements.

On October 16, U.N. Secretary-General Boutros-Ghali telephoned Savimbi to inform him personally that, although the MPLA had won a majority in the legislative elections, there was not a presidential majority and that a run-

---

[1] For the U.N.'s own account of its efforts, see. United Nations Department of Public Information, Reference Paper, "The United Nations and the Situation in Angola, May 1991-June 1994," (undated).

[2] UNAVEM II was created on May 30, 1991 for a period of seventeen months, until October 31, 1992. Since then, the U.N. Security Council has extended UNAVEM's mandate twelve times: SCR 785 (October 30, 1992) to November 30, 1992; SCR 793 (November 30, 1992) to January 31, 1993; SCR 804 (January 29, 1993) to April 30, 1993; SCR 823 (April 30, 1993) to May 31, 1993; SCR 834 (June 1, 1993) to July 15, 1993; SCR 851 (July 15, 1993) to September 15, 1993; SCR 864 (September 15, 1993) to December 15, 1993; SCR 890 (December 15, 1993) to March 15, 1994; SCR 903 (March 16, 1994) to May 31, 1994; SCR 922 (May 31, 1994) to June 30, 1994; SCR 932 (June 30, 1994) to September 30, 1994; and, SCR 945 (September 29, 1994) to October 31, 1994.

off was required which under Angolan electoral law had to be within thirty days. The National Electoral Council announced the results the following day. Immediately after this announcement UNITA stepped up its nationwide campaign to occupy municipalities by force and remove government administrative structures. In several incidents government administrators were killed; in others they had to flee or were evicted.

On October 20, the Troika representatives met with both Savimbi and President dos Santos in separate sessions urging them to meet face to face. Savimbi maintained that the elections were a blatant fraud and that he was the only person in his organization who believed in a second round of voting, but he nevertheless agreed to participate in a presidential runoff. The following day government and UNITA representatives met in Luanda for extended discussions on the technicalities of a presidential runoff.

Meanwhile there had been outbreaks of fighting in Huambo on October 17-18. In October 30 and November 1 fighting broke out in Luanda and in various other cities across the country. U.N. and foreign diplomats were eventually able to broker a ceasefire on November 2. The U.N. Under Secretary for Peacekeeping Operations, Marrack Goulding, followed this up on a November 6-12 mission to assess the role of UNAVEM and investigate how to resume the peace process. Meanwhile UNITA troops were reported to have left the designated containment areas across the country.

A diplomatic initiative by South Africa at this juncture broke ranks and undermined the diplomacy of the U.N. and the Troika. Foreign Minister Pik Botha spent time in Luanda and Huambo in mid-October trying to bring about a Savimbi-dos Santos summit. The South Africans also encouraged UNITA to propose a power-sharing deal in which Angola would shift from a unitary state to a federation. On November 9 the Angolan government declared Pik Botha persona non grata, ending South African mediation attempts.

NAMIBE TALKS

Following the South African failure, Margaret Anstee held talks with Savimbi on November 24 and with President dos Santos the following day, obtaining agreement for the first high-level encounter between the two sides since October 31, the day fighting broke out in Luanda. The result was U.N.-sponsored talks on November 26 in Namibe province between the government and UNITA. These produced a declaration signed by both sides that they would fully implement the Bicesse accords, observe a nationwide ceasefire, terminate offensive troop movements, and permit expansion of U.N. involvement in the process. However, within days UNITA forces invalidated the agreement by occupying the northern cities of Uíge and Negage.

In December, U.N. representatives made three visits to Uíge, trying to negotiate a withdrawal with UNITA's General Dembo. Arrangements were finalized on a UNITA withdrawal on December 27, and the government sent two officers and about 200 FAA troops to prepare for the reinstatement of government administration.

Meanwhile other mediation attempts continued. On December 15, UNITA issued an eleven-point plan to get the peace process back on course. On December 20, Jeffrey Davidow, then U.S. Deputy Assistant Secretary of State for African Affairs, visited Huambo to meet Savimbi to urge him to resume peace negotiations. On January 2, 1993 Margaret Anstee met with Savimbi in Huambo and, later the same day, met with government officials in Luanda. Both sides indicated their intention to proceed with a second Namibe meeting, provided the Uíge/Negage problem was resolved.

This promising development was cut short by renewed warfare. Starting in Lubango on January 3, it quickly spread to other provincial capitals and towns as government forces purged UNITA supporters. In a report to the Security Council, Secretary-General Boutros-Ghali stated on January 21 that "Angola had returned to civil war."

In addition, U.N. Security Council Resolution 804 of January 29, 1993, singled out UNITA for the first time for particular criticism, stating that the Security Council "[u]rges once again the two parties, and in particular UNITA, to produce early evidence of their adherence to and fulfillment without exception of, 'Acordos de Paz.'"

ADDIS ABABA TALKS

U.N.-mediated peace talks between the Angolan government and UNITA in Addis Ababa, Ethiopia, on January 28-30, 1993 achieved little, except to identify the key issues blocking progress towards a ceasefire. UNITA canceled a second round of negotiations with the Angolan government scheduled for February 10 in Addis Ababa, claiming that its delegation could not leave Angola because of the Huambo fighting. On February 14, Portugal, Russia and the U.S., the three co-signatories of the Bicesse Accords, issued an ultimatum to UNITA, giving it three days to return to the negotiating table. If this did not happen, they said, they would "not fail to draw the necessary conclusions." At the end of three days they extended the ultimatum by two more days. UNITA finally agreed to meet with the Angolan government in Addis Ababa on February 26. But in spite of an extended March 1 deadline, UNITA failed to appear for talks in Addis and U.N. officials canceled the talks. Since UNAVEM had put its own transport and communications facilities at the disposal of the UNITA delegation, it was clear that UNITA wanted to recapture Huambo from the government before it re-entered negotiations. On March 8, Huambo fell to UNITA.

On March 10, Jonas Savimbi, emboldened by his military success in Huambo, demanded U.N. Special Representative Margaret Anstee's removal and made extreme accusations against her. Savimbi alleged that Anstee was partisan in favor of the Angolan government, and stated that UNITA would not participate in any further peace talks negotiated by her. The following day Boutros-Ghali expressed his support for Anstee and reiterated his warning that the U.N. would withdraw from Angola when its mandate expired at the end of April unless significant progress was reached in ending the conflict. UNAVEM was unable to obtain a truce which would have enabled relief organizations to deliver food and medicine to the thousands of wounded and besieged civilians in Huambo.

ABIDJAN TALKS

Between March 25-29, 1993, bilateral talks aimed at finding a peaceful solution were held in Abidjan, Ivory Coast, between the U.S. and UNITA. An Angolan government delegation was also at hand for informal consultations with the U.S. delegation, but did not take part in the talks. UNITA and the government then agreed to return to U.N.-chaired peace talks, which began on April 12. Boutros-Ghali tried to keep the pressure on Savimbi by writing to him on April 14 to urge him to move ahead in the negotiations. After several suspensions due to tit-for-tat delaying tactics by the Angolan government and UNITA there appeared to be progress when Savimbi announced on April 27, following talks with Ivory Coast Foreign Minister Amara Essy, that he agreed to a ceasefire. Although this ended a dispute over whether there should be a "cessation of hostilities" or a formal ceasefire, new disagreements caused the talks once again to collapse on May 21.

Agreement had been reached on a power-sharing formula in the draft, thirty-eight point Abidjan Protocol. This Protocol covered every aspect of the conflict, ranging from the cessation of hostilities and the cantonment of troops to the second round of elections. But UNITA refused to agree to Article 11 of the draft peace protocol which required UNITA fighters to withdraw from areas illegally occupied since fighting broke out in October 1992. The philosophy underlying the negotiations was that political concessions by the government were to be made in exchange for military concessions by UNITA. At the time, UNITA controlled about 75 percent of the national territory and the government was anxious to have an agreement.

During the talks both UNITA and the Angolan government called for an enlargement of UNAVEM II's mandate, arguing that the U.N. should set up an "intervention force." UNITA also asked for U.N. troops to be deployed in any locations from which UNITA withdrew to ensure the safety of UNITA supporters. Margaret Anstee supported this by trying to secure U.N. support for a small contingent of "Blue Helmets" to be sent to Angola. She later concluded that the Abidjan process possibly failed because she was unable to obtain a U.N. commitment on this deployment. She commented:

> One of the ironies in Abidjan was that both sides had agreed, virtually in toto, to a blueprint for what will be called UNAVEM III, to support the implementation of the Abidjan Protocol once it was signed. UNAVEM III was to have a greatly increased mandate and resources to match; the aim, in effect, was to repair all the shortcomings of the mandate of UNAVEM II. Moreover, we understood informally that the Security Council was ready to authorize such a transformation once a ceasefire was agreed. So we had a "chicken and egg" situation. The Security Council required agreement at Abidjan before "Blue Helmets" could be considered. UNITA wanted assurance of at least an immediate, symbolic presence of Blue Helmets before they would agree to the terms for a ceasefire set out in the Abidjan Protocol. The reality was even worse than that. I was told that I must warn both sides, that even if they agreed to a ceasefire, no U.N. troops could, for practical reasons, be made available until six to nine months later. Not surprisingly, I had two nightmares in Abidjan: one was that I would fail, which is what happened; the other was that I would succeed because then I could not see how a ceasefire would be monitored and supported.[3]

---

[3] Margaret Anstee, "Angola: The Forgotten Tragedy, A Test Case for U.N. Peacekeeping," *International Relations*, Vol. XI, No. 6, December 1993, p.502.

On May 19, 1993, the Clinton administration recognized the Angolan government. The new administration, which took office in January 1993, had been withholding recognition in the hope that this would give it extra leverage over UNITA. However, increasing frustration at UNITA's continued intransigence in the Abidjan talks and intelligence assessments suggesting that UNITA was unable to achieve military victory by capturing Luanda helped persuade the Clinton administration to recognize the MPLA-dominated government. While U.S. recognition of the Angolan government increased UNITA's isolation, Savimbi had already begun in late March to warn his supporters to expect U.S. recognition.

The U.N. Security Council passed another resolution (SCR 823) on April 30. It reaffirmed past resolutions and extended UNAVEM's mandate until May 31, 1993. The Security Council also condemned attacks on international humanitarian flights, particularly by UNITA, which had shot down a World Food Program aircraft in eastern Angola on April 26. UNITA was trying to cut off delivery of food aid to isolated government-held towns in order to capture them. At the same time UNAVEM further reduced its presence to Luanda, Sumbe (Cuanza Sul), Namibe (Namibe), Lubango (Huíla) and Benguela (Benguela).

A draft resolution on the extension of UNAVEM's mandate for a further sixty days, with reduced staff, was not adopted as expected, because of disagreement within the Security Council. UNAVEM's mandate expired on May 31, 1993, but was renewed by a compromise resolution on June 1 (SCR 834) which extended the mandate for forty-five days to July 15 and retained UNAVEM's staffing levels at the Secretary-General's discretion. SCR 834 also held UNITA "responsible for the breakdown of the [Abidjan] talks and for thereby jeopardizing the peace process."

Margaret Anstee, in New York for the Security Council debates, lobbied for but failed to secure immediate U.N. Security Council authority for armed U.N. troops to escort food and medical supplies along neutral humanitarian aid corridors. Anstee had already appealed to both President dos Santos and Savimbi to open up ten air corridors and four land-based corridors to distribute badly needed aid across the country. An estimated 1,000 Angolans a day were dying at the time.

Although Margaret Anstee previously indicated several times her desire to retire, the U.N. Secretary General encouraged her to remain in her post until the peace process was back on track. Following the collapse of the Abidjan talks Anstee was at last allowed to retire. Her replacement, former Malian Foreign Minister Alioune Blondin Beye was appointed on June 28. Beye, director of the legal department of the African Development Bank based in Ivory Coast, had twice been a candidate for secretary-general of the Organization of African Unity. Boutros-Ghali had in fact tagged Sérgio Vieira de Mello, the Brazilian-born representative for the U.N. High Commissioner for Refugees in Cambodia, for the job, but UNITA opposed his nomination on the grounds that he came from Brazil, which they accused of being too friendly with the Angolan government.

Beye inherited a peace process in tatters. On August 4, Savimbi's birthday festivities in Huambo were disrupted by government bombing raids. Meanwhile, fighting intensified in Kuito, raising speculation that UNITA was trying to capture the city for Savimbi's birthday.

Movement toward new talks occurred on August 11 when Savimbi called for unconditional peace talks with the government. On August 20, Beye received an oral message from Savimbi, delivered by a special envoy from President Mobutu of Zaire, reiterating his call for an "immediate ceasefire without conditions." Beye requested a meeting with Savimbi to pursue this, and various other international initiatives also took place in this period in an attempt to promote renewed dialogue between the government and UNITA.

King Hassan of Morocco, President Houphouet-Boigny of the Ivory Coast and African National Congress president Nelson Mandela attempted to bring about a face-to-face meeting between Savimbi and President dos Santos, but this initiative was blocked by the Angolan government. An attempt to talk with Savimbi by the OAU Ad Hoc Committee on Southern Africa, headed by President Mugabe of Zimbabwe, fell through when Huambo, UNITA's suggested location for the meeting, was unacceptable to the Ad Hoc Committee. All attempts to persuade Savimbi to leave Angola for talks with the U.N. Special Representative and other mediators failed, with UNITA claiming that security considerations made this impossible. The U.N. sought permission to deploy peacekeeping troops in local ceasefires to help humanitarian initiatives, especially in Kuito, Malanje and Menongue. The government rejected these efforts, arguing that peacekeeping forces should operate only in the context of a comprehensive ceasefire within the framework of the Abidjan Protocol.

On September 15, 1993 the U.N. Security Council adopted Resolution 864, invoking Chapter VII of the U.N. Charter and imposing sanctions on the sale of weapons and petroleum to UNITA, effective September 25, 1993. The threat of these sanctions appeared to yield results. Following a meeting in Huambo of its senior leadership UNITA announced a unilateral ceasefire on September 20. Although the fighting did not stop completely, it subsided for several months.

As the U.N. sanctions against UNITA took effect, Beye and other foreign diplomats met with a high-ranking UNITA delegation in São Tomé. This meeting was boycotted by the Angolan government. Following the São Tome meeting, UNITA's Central Committee issued a communique on October 6 restating the set of principles agreed to in Abidjan, but for the first time accepting the principle of withdrawing its forces from urban areas to cantonment areas.

LUSAKA TALKS

These diplomatic initiatives led to both sides agreeing to participate in yet another round of peace talks, which began on November 15, 1993, chaired by U.N. Special Representative Beye with the participation of the U.S. Special Representative to the Angolan Peace Process, Ambassador Paul Hare, and observers from Russia and Portugal. The closed door negotiations included a timetable for a ceasefire and UNITA troop demobilization, and a formula for national reconciliation between the two parties. Following clear progress on military issues in the peace talks the government presented to Beye on December 13 its proposal for a national reconciliation government.

Soon thereafter, the Lusaka talks broke for consultations in the wake of allegations that the government had bombed Kuito where it was rumored Savimbi was attending a soccer match. Talks resumed in early January 1994, with the government and UNITA negotiators agreeing on January 31 on the composition of both the police and anti-riot units. The talks progressed slowly, with the pace determined by calculations on each side of the battlefield advantages. The timetable following the signing of an agreement in Lusaka was however agreed upon. Under this plan the U.N. Security Council would meet to authorize the deployment of a U.N. military force for Angola under the auspices of UNAVEM III. The plan calls for the deployment of a comprehensive UNAVEM III force as follows:

1. Within ten days, 100 U.N. military troops will be sent to Angola;
2. Within thirty days, 350 additional troops and 126 police observers along with 14 medical personnel will be deployed; and,
3. Within sixty to ninety days, approximately 6,000 troops will be dispatched to Angola as part of the overall Lusaka Accord.

In addition, representatives of the Angolan government and UNITA were to meet in São Tomé & Príncipe under U.N. auspices within ten days following the initialing of the Lusaka Accords to finalize the details of the military and police framework agreed on in Lusaka. Only five days were allotted for this complicated and detailed process. An official signing ceremony, possibly carried out by President dos Santos and Savimbi, would occur within thirty days of the initialling of the accord.

Despite this appearance of progress the talks bogged down in discussions on power-sharing. On March 6, 1994, the government restated its December 13 proposal with only slight revisions. UNITA responded with counter-proposals on March 10 and again on March 17. This resulted in deadlock and a recess was called. Beye travelled to Huambo on March 12 to see Savimbi and to Switzerland on April 6 to consult the U.N. Secretary-General Boutros-Ghali.

In late April the U.S. intervened. President Clinton sent two letters to President dos Santos urging him to accept a compromise package drawn up by the mediators in Lusaka. On May 25, President dos Santos finally responded by accepting the mediator's package. But any optimism that a deal was imminent vanished on June 8 after UNITA's delegation in Lusaka presented its response to the mediation proposals on power sharing. These proposals offered UNITA four ministerial posts, seven vice-ministerial posts, six ambassadorships, thirty municipal administrators, thirty-five vice-municipal administrators and seventy-five local administrators. UNITA accepted three provincial governorships suggested by the mediation but added Huambo and requested that the vice-governorship of Huambo offered to them be swapped for Malanje and that an ambassadorial post in Mexico should be swapped for one in Germany. UNITA told the mediators, "The addition of Huambo to the list of provinces to be administered by UNITA is fundamental. To ignore the logic of this request is to close one's eyes to the reality of conflict resolution."

As neither side would compromise over the Huambo issue, U.N. Special Representative Beye, accompanied by representatives of the three observer states, travelled to Huambo on June 18 for talks with Savimbi on this sticking point. On June 23 they went on to Cape Town, South Africa, to meet President Mandela. Beye also held meetings with President dos Santos (June 19 and July 13), and several other African leaders, including President Chiluba of Zambia (June 28), President Mugabe of Zimbabwe (July 1) and President Mobutu of Zaire (July 12). His objective was to secure help in the Lusaka talks in resolving the issue of UNITA's participation in the future state administration of Angola, especially the Huambo governorship.

On July 7, President Mandela hosted a summit meeting in Pretoria attended by the presidents of Angola, Mozambique and Zaire, during which it was decided to revive a long dormant, and often only symbolic, Security Commission between Angola and Zaire. At the meeting it was revealed that President Mandela had invited Savimbi to visit South Africa. On July 5, President Chiluba visited Luanda for talks with President dos Santos. The following day, a high-level delegation from the Zambian ruling party travelled to Huambo to talk to Savimbi. It tried to table compromise initiatives over the governorship of Huambo, including a suggestion that it should be held by a neutral from another party. The government rejected these proposals.

Developments in September gave reason for hope. UNITA sent a letter to the Security Council on September 5 which the Council declared "constituted the required formal acceptance by UNITA of the complete set of proposals on national reconciliation put forth in the Lusaka peace talks." The Security Council stated that as a result, it would not consider imposition of additional measures against UNITA, indicated in S.C. Resolution 864 (1993), i.e., trade sanctions and travel restrictions in addition to the arms and oil embargo. The Security Council declared, "The way is now clear for an early conclusion of the negotiations in Lusaka towards a comprehensive agreement within the framework of the 'Acordos de Paz' and relevant Security Council resolutions. It urges both parties to reach such an agreement before the expiry of the present mandate of UNAVEM II on 30 September 1994."[4]

On September 29, 1994, the Security Council unanimously adopted Resolution 945, extending the mandate of UNAVEM II until October 31, 1994. The Security Council also stated "its grave concern over the continuation of military hostilities throughout the territory of Angola, which cause extensive suffering to the civilian population and hamper the successful conclusion of the Lusaka Peace Talks..."[5] In Lusaka on October 17, negotiators for the government and UNITA announced agreement on a comprehensive peace treaty, pending approval by leaders in Angola. It appears that both sides are pressing forward on the diplomatic track while preparing militarily for a breakdown in the peace process.

---

[4] Press statement, SC/5899, U.N. Security Council, 3423rd Meeting (PM), September 9, 1994. The official document is S/PRST/1994/52.

[5] SC/5907, U.N. Security Council, 3431st Meeting, Night Summary, September 29, 1994.

U.S. POLICY[6]

The Clinton administration initially delayed recognizing the Angolan government in the hope that this would give it extra leverage over UNITA. The State Department was divided at the time, with some officers arguing that prompt recognition following the elections would give a clear message to UNITA that the U.S. fully supported the democratic process. Others hoped to draw UNITA back into the political process by delaying recognition until the electoral run-off.

There is little evidence that the leverage of recognition was used to extract human rights concessions from Luanda, or that delaying recognition was employed to encourage comparable improvements from UNITA in this respect. Eventually, increasing frustration at UNITA's continued intransigence convinced the administration to recognize the Angolan government on May 19, 1993. But by then, the country was immersed in full-scale civil war, with thousands of civilians being killed by the warring parties.

Soon after recognition, the U.S. upgraded its Luanda liaison office to embassy status and appointed its first ambassador. The U.S. arms embargo was lifted in June 1993, with the understanding that only non-lethal equipment would be provided.[7] Thus far, shipments have apparently been limited to items used in humanitarian operations.

With the exception of official recognition of the government, U.S. policy under the Clinton administration has changed little from U.S. policy at the end of the Bush administration. In 1993, Robert Cabelly, then a special advisor to Assistant Secretary of State for African Affairs George Moose, drafted a policy document on Angola, which essentially articulated existing policy: the United States would substitute political initiatives for its previous

---

[6] See also Human Rights Watch, "Human Rights in Africa and U.S. Policy: A Special Report By Human Rights Watch/Africa for the White House Conference on Africa," June 26-27, 1994.

[7] The Department of State terminated the domestic arms embargo against Angola effective July 2, 1993. Section 126.1(a) of the International Traffic in Arms Regulations (ITAR) was amended to reflect this change of policy. The U.S. government now reviews all licenses and approves exports on a case-to-case basis, with a presumption of denial for lethal articles. See *Federal Register Notice*, Vol.58, No.126, page 35864, July 2, 1993.

policy of arming UNITA, and encourage both sides to return to peace talks. At the urging of key members of Congress, the administration in late October appointed a special envoy to assist U.N. peace efforts and attend the talks that began that month in Lusaka.

Apparently fearing that public attention to human rights abuses by the government and UNITA might jeopardize the peace process, the State Department largely has kept silent about human rights and violations of the laws of war in Angola. Testimony before Congress over the past two years has concentrated on developments in the peace process and on humanitarian concerns, but there has been little public censure of the warring parties for abuses against noncombatants. The resurgence of hostilities in 1994 has led to growing coolness between the U.S. and the government. Luanda in return appears to be increasingly critical of international mediation efforts.

Assistant Secretary of State George Moose, unlike his predecessors since the Carter administration, appears to have distanced himself deliberately from Angola policy. His absence from the Angolan government's celebration of the presentation of credentials of its first ambassador to Washington was a diplomatic signal that was widely noted in Washington. Angola policy appears to have been delegated to the director of the Southern Africa Office, April Glaspie, though Glaspie herself has openly said that she spends little time on Angolan issues. It was Congress, in response to this perceived passivity on Angola, which encouraged the appointment of a special presidential envoy. The subsequent appointment of Ambassador Paul Hare in October suggests that Angola may now be getting more attention within the Clinton administration.

U.S. policy in Angola during 1994 has so far remained focused on the slow and tortuous peace talks taking place in Lusaka, Zambia. In an attempt to push the process forward, President Clinton, on advice from Ambassador Hare, sent two letters, in April and in May, to President dos Santos, urging the Angolan president to accept the proposals put forward by the mediators. President dos Santos replied on May 27, agreeing to the proposals but adding a list of his government's conditions. These conditions also were discussed by the Angolan president and a fact-finding delegation of U.S. Senators, led by Senator Paul Simon, Chairman of the Senate Foreign Relations Subcommittee on Africa. President Clinton sent a letter in early June to Savimbi urging him to accept the Angolan government's offer of positions in central, provincial, and local administrations. The U.S. continues to promote a diplomatic settlement.

VIII. APPLICATION OF THE LAWS OF WAR TO THE ANGOLAN CONFLICT

The conduct of government armies and insurgent forces in an internal conflict is expressly regulated by the rules of war, also called international humanitarian law, which comprise the four 1949 Geneva Conventions, the two 1977 Protocols to those conventions, and the customary laws of war. Unlike human rights law, humanitarian law was developed to meet the particular exigencies of armed conflicts and their basic provisions are not derogable nor capable of suspension. The rules are primarily intended to protect the victims of armed conflicts. Unlike human rights law, which specifically applies to governments, humanitarian law applies to all parties to armed conflicts. Governments continue to be bound by the basic standards of human rights law that can never be suspended even in times of emergency.

Despite their separate origins and fields of application, human rights and international humanitarian law share the common purpose of securing for all persons a minimum standard of treatment under all circumstances. For example, both human rights and humanitarian law conventions absolutely prohibit summary executions, torture and other inhuman treatment, and the application of *ex-post facto* law.

A NEW NON-INTERNATIONAL ARMED CONFLICT

International humanitarian law makes a critical distinction between international and non-international (internal) armed conflicts. Since the rules governing each type of conflict vary significantly, a proper characterization of the conflict is necessary to determine which aspects of humanitarian law apply.

The nature of the conflict in Angola has changed radically since October 1992. Before the Bicesse Accords of May 1991 the armed conflict in Angola was an example of an "internationalized" non-international conflict, a civil war characterized by the intervention of the armed forces of other states on behalf of opposing parties to the civil war. This is apparently no longer the case.

Since the resumption of hostilities after the 1992 elections, no state has either declared war against Angola or is known to have directly intervened with its forces against the government. Thus, the requisite preconditions for the existence of an international armed conflict are not clearly satisfied at this time.[1] With respect to Zaire, the apparent involvement of some Zairian soldiers in support of UNITA reflects a decades-long tradition of cross-border assistance to opponents of the Angolan government. However, the exact nature and extent of military cooperation between Zaire and UNITA is unclear.

The nature of hostilities between the government of Angola and UNITA, then, allows the application of the standards applicable to a non-international armed conflict. As such, government and insurgent forces' conduct is governed by common Article 3 to the four 1949 Geneva Conventions and by customary international law applicable to internal armed conflicts. The 1977 Protocol II to the Geneva Conventions contains rules providing authoritative guidance on the conduct of hostilities by the warring parties.[2]

THE APPLICATION OF ARTICLE 3

Article 3 which is common to the four Geneva Conventions[3] is virtually a convention within a convention. It is the only provision of the Geneva Conventions that directly applies to internal (as opposed to international) conflicts. Common Article 3, section 1, states:

> In the case of armed conflict not of an international character occurring in the territory of one of the High Contracting Parties, each Party to the conflict shall be bound to apply, as a minimum, the following provisions:

---

[1] Under Article 2 common to the four 1949 Geneva Conventions, an international armed conflict must involve a declared war or any other armed conflict which might arise "between two or more of the High Contracting Parties" to the Convention; it is also described as any difference between two states leading to the intervention of armed forces. Only states and not rebel groups may be "High Contracting Parties."

[2] Angola has not ratified Protocol II.

[3] Angola acceded to the four Geneva Conventions and Protocol I thereto on September 20, 1984, and is therefore a High Contracting Party.

(1) Persons taking no active part in the hostilities, including members of armed forces who have laid down their arms and those placed *hors de combat* by sickness, wounds, detention, or any other cause, shall in all circumstances be treated humanely, without any adverse distinction founded on race, color, religion or faith, sex, birth or wealth, or any other similar criteria.

To this end the following acts are and shall remain prohibited at any time and in any place whatsoever with respect to the above-mentioned persons:

(a) violence to life and person, in particular murder of all kinds, mutilation, cruel treatment and torture;

(b) taking of hostages;

(c) outrages upon personal dignity, in particular humiliating and degrading treatment;

(d) the passing of sentences and the carrying out of executions without previous judgment pronounced by a regularly constituted court, affording all the judicial guarantees which are recognized as indispensable by civilized peoples.

Article 3 thus imposes fixed legal obligations on the parties to an internal conflict to ensure humane treatment of persons not, or no longer, taking an active role in the hostilities. It applies when a situation of internal armed conflict objectively exists in the territory of a State Party and expressly binds all parties to the internal conflict, including insurgents, even though they do not have the legal capacity to sign the Geneva Conventions. In Angola, the government and UNITA are parties to the conflict.

The obligation to apply Article 3 is absolute for all parties to the conflict and independent of the obligation of the other parties. That means that the Angolan government cannot excuse itself from complying with Article 3 on the grounds that UNITA is violating Article 3, and vice versa. In addition, application of Article 3 by the government cannot be legally construed as recognition of the insurgent party's belligerence, from which recognition of additional legal obligations beyond common Article 3 would flow. Nor is it necessary for any government to recognize UNITA's belligerent status for Article 3 to apply.

Unlike international conflicts, the law governing internal armed conflicts does not recognize the combatant's privilege[4] and therefore does not provide any special status for combatants, even when captured. Thus, the Angolan government is not obliged to grant captured members of UNITA prisoner of war status and since UNITA forces are not privileged combatants, they may be tried and punished by the Angolan government for treason, sedition, and the commission of other crimes under domestic laws. Similarly, government army combatants who are captured by UNITA need not be accorded prisoner of war status. Any party may agree to treat its captives as prisoners of war, however.

CUSTOMARY INTERNATIONAL LAW APPLICABLE TO INTERNAL ARMED CONFLICTS

United Nations General Assembly Resolution 2444[5] expressly recognized the customary law principle of civilian immunity and its complementary principle requiring the warring parties to distinguish civilians from combatants at all times. The preamble to this resolution states that these fundamental humanitarian law principles apply "in all armed conflicts," meaning both international and internal armed conflicts. Resolution 2444 affirms:

> ...the following principles for observance by all government and other authorities responsible for action in armed conflicts:

---

[4] The combatant's privilege is a license to "kill or capture enemy troops, destroy military objectives and cause unavoidable civilian casualties." This privilege immunizes members of armed forces or rebels from criminal prosecution by their captors for their violent acts that do not violate the laws of war but would otherwise be crimes under domestic law. Prisoner of war status depends on and flows from this privilege. See Solf, "The Status of Combatants in Non-International Armed Conflicts Under Domestic Law and Transnational Practice," *American University Law Review* 33 (1953), p. 59.

[5] U.N. General Assembly, *Respect for Human Rights in Armed Conflicts*, United Nations General Assembly Resolution 2444, 23 UN GAOR Supp. (No.18), p. 164, UN. Doc. A/7433 (New York: U.N., 1968).

(a) That the right of the parties to a conflict to adopt means of injuring the enemy is not unlimited;

(b) That it is prohibited to launch attacks against the civilian population as such;

(c) That distinction must be made at all times between persons taking part in the hostilities and members of the civilian population to the effect that the latter be spared as much as possible.

PROTECTION OF THE CIVILIAN POPULATION UNDER THE RULES OF WAR

In situations of internal conflict, generally speaking, a civilian is anyone who is not a member of the armed forces or of an organized armed group of a party to the conflict. Accordingly, "the civilian population comprises all persons who do not actively participate in the hostilities."[6]

Civilians may not be subject to deliberate individualized attack since they pose no immediate threat to the adversary.[7] The term "civilian" also includes some employees of the military establishment who are not members of the armed forces but assist them.[8] While as civilians they may not be targeted, these civilian employees of military establishments or those who indirectly assist

---

[6] R. Goldman, "International Humanitarian Law and the Armed Conflicts in El Salvador and Nicaragua," *American University Journal of International Law & Policy* 2 (1987): p. 553.

[7] Michael Bothe, Karl Josef Partsch, Waldeman A. Solf, *New Rules for Victims of Armed Conflicts* (The Hague: Martinus Nijhoff Publishers, 1982), p. 303.

[8] Civilians include those persons who are "directly linked to the armed forces, including those who accompany the armed forces without being members thereof, such as civilian members of military aircraft crews, supply contractors, members of labor units, or of services responsible for the welfare of the armed forces, members of the crew of the merchant marine and the crews of civil aircraft employed in the transportation of military personnel, material or supplies . . . . Civilians employed in the production, distribution and storage of munitions of war . . . ." *Ibid.*, pp. 293-94.

combatants assume the risk of death or injury incidental to attacks against legitimate military targets while they are at or in the immediate vicinity of military targets.

Persons protected by Article 3 include members of both government and UNITA forces who surrender, are wounded, sick, or are captured. They are *hors de combat*, literally, out of combat, until such time as they take a hostile action such as attempting to escape.

DESIGNATION OF MILITARY OBJECTIVES

Under the laws of war, military objectives are defined only as they relate to objects or targets, rather than to personnel. To constitute a legitimate military objective, the object or target, selected by its nature, location, purpose, or use, must contribute effectively to the enemy's military capability or activity, and its total or partial destruction or neutralization must offer a definite military advantage in the circumstances.[9]

Legitimate military objectives are combatants' weapons, convoys, installations, and supplies. In addition:

> an object generally used for civilian purposes, such as a
> dwelling, a bus, a fleet of taxicabs, or a civilian airfield or
> railroad siding, can become a military objective if its location
> or use meets [the criteria in Protocol I, Art. 52(2)].[10]

Members of the Angolan government's armed forces and UNITA are legitimate military targets and subject to attack, individually or collectively, until such time as they become *hors de combat*, that is, surrender or are wounded or captured.[11] Government-sponsored militia are also proper military targets while they directly participate in hostilities.

---

[9] Protocol I, Art. 52 (2).

[10] Bothe, *New Rules for Victims of Armed Conflicts*, pp. 306-07.

[11] Killing a wounded or captured combatant is not proper because it does not offer a "definite military advantage in the circumstances" because the fighter is already rendered useless or *hors de combat*.

PROHIBITED ACTS

While not an all-encompassing list, customary and conventional international law prohibits the following kinds of practices, orders, or actions:

● Orders that there shall be no survivors, such threats to combatants, or direction to conduct hostilities on this basis.

● Attacks against combatants who are captured, surrender, or are placed *hors de combat*.

● Torture, any form of corporal punishment, or other cruel treatment of persons under any circumstances.

● Desecration of corpses.[12] Mutilation of the dead is never permissible and violates the rules of war.

● The infliction of humiliating or degrading treatment on civilians or combatants who are captured, have surrendered, or are otherwise *hors de combat*.

● Hostage taking.[13]

● Shielding. This prohibits using the presence of the civilian population to immunize legitimate military targets from attack or areas from military operations, or to favor or impede military operations.[14]

---

[12] Protocol II, Article 8, states: "Whenever circumstances permit, and particularly after an engagement, all possible measures shall be taken, without delay....to search for the dead, prevent their being despoiled, and decently dispose of them."

[13] One authority defines hostages as persons who find themselves, willingly or unwillingly, in the power of the enemy and who answer with their freedom or their life for compliance with the orders of the latter and for upholding the security of its armed forces. ICRC, *Commentary on the Additional Protocols,* p. 874.

[14] See Protocol I, Article 51 (7).

• Pillage and destruction of civilian property. This prohibition is designed to spare civilians the suffering resulting from the destruction of their real and personal property: houses, furniture, clothing, provisions, tools, and so forth. Pillage includes organized acts as well as individual acts without the consent of the military authorities.[15]

TAXATION OR FOOD REQUISITION

There is little authority in international law for a rebel army fighting in an internal conflict to requisition property from the civilian population or to impose taxes upon them. These acts of authority are usually regarded as being those of the power which a state can exert over its own citizens and others residing in their territory. A rebel army is not a State and does not have all the powers of States vis-a-vis those who reside under its military jurisdiction.

In an international armed conflict, a State army that occupies territory of another State has certain limited powers to requisition food from the population in that territory. That occupying power is, however, required to ensure the food and medical supplies of the population first, and must bring in the necessary food and other articles if the resources of the occupied territory are inadequate. The occupying power may only requisition food if the requirements of the civilian population have been taken into account. Then the occupying power must make arrangements to pay fair value for the requisitioned goods.[16]

A noted authority comments, "During recent conflicts thousands of human beings suffered from starvation during the occupation of the country. Their destruction was made still worse by requisitioning."[17] The above provisions in the 1949 Geneva Conventions were designed to prevent such destitution.

Common Article 3 to the four 1949 Geneva Conventions and Protocol II, which pertain to internal armed conflicts, do not specifically empower the

---

[15] ICRC, *Commentary, IV Geneva Convention* (Geneva: ICRC, 1958), p. 226.

[16] IV Geneva Convention of 1949, art. 55. These limitations and restrictions were specifically not imposed on the relations between a State party and its own residents or citizens.

[17] ICRC, *Commentary, IV Geneva Convention*, p. 309.

rebel army to requisition food or other articles, or to tax civilians. And even if such authority to requisition or tax existed, there is no reason why it should be superior to the authority conferred on occupying powers under IV Geneva, Article 55. In almost every respect, a rebel army and its combatants in an internal conflict have fewer humanitarian law rights than does a State party to an international conflict.[18] But even if the rebel army does have rights comparable to those of the occupying power to requisition food from the civilian population as described in IV Geneva, Article 55, then the extent and methods of UNITA's requisition of food from the civilian population must also be deemed to be a violation of Article 55. The occupying power may under no circumstances take food from the population without taking the needs of the civilian population into account. In the case of civilians subjected to food requisition by UNITA and the government, they are often unable to meet their own minimal subsistence needs, let alone have a surplus for an army.

PROHIBITION ON INDISCRIMINATE ATTACKS: THE PRINCIPLE OF PROPORTIONALITY

The civilian population and individual civilians in general are to be protected against attack. As noted above, any target must constitute a legitimate military object, which means it must: (1) contribute effectively to the enemy's military capability or activity, and (2) its total or partial destruction or neutralization must offer a definite military advantage in the circumstances.

The laws of war implicitly characterize all objects as civilian unless they satisfy this two-fold test. Objects normally dedicated to civilian use, such as churches, houses and schools, are presumed not to be military objectives. If, in fact, they do assist the enemy's military action, they can then lose their immunity from direct attack. This presumption attaches, however, only to objects that ordinarily have no significant military use or purpose. For example, this presumption would not include objects such as transportation and communication systems that under applicable criteria are military objectives.

The attacker must also do everything feasible to verify that the objectives to be attacked are not civilian. "Feasible" means "that which is

---

[18] For example, in an internal conflict there is no combatant's privilege and thus captured combatants do not have the status of prisoners of war. In an international conflict, captured combatants have extensive rights and protections detailed in III Geneva Convention.

practical or practically possible taking into account all the circumstances at the time, including those relevant to the success of military operations."[19]

Even attacks on legitimate military targets are, however, limited by the principle of proportionality. This principle places a duty on combatants to choose means of attack that avoid or minimize damage to civilians. In particular, the attacker should refrain from launching an attack if the expected civilian casualties would outweigh the importance of the military target to the attacker. The principle of proportionality is codified in Protocol I, Article 51 (5):

> Among others, the following types of attacks are to be considered as indiscriminate:...
> (b) an attack which may be expected to cause incidental loss of civilian life, injury to civilians, damage to civilian objects, or combination thereof, which would be excessive in relation to the concrete and direct military advantage anticipated.
> If an attack can be expected to cause incidental civilian casualties or damage, two requirements must be met before that attack is launched. First, there must be an anticipated "concrete and direct" military advantage. "Direct" means "without intervening condition or agency"... A remote advantage to be gained at some unknown time in the future would not be a proper consideration to weigh against civilian losses.[20]

Creating conditions "conducive to surrender by means of attacks which incidentally harm the civilian population"[21] is too remote and insufficiently military to qualify as a "concrete and direct" military advantage. "A military advantage can only consist in ground gained and in annihilation or weakening the enemy armed forces."[22] The "concrete and direct" military advantage surpasses the "definite" military advantage required to qualify an object or target as a "legitimate military target."

---

[19] Bothe, *New Rules for Victims of Armed Conflict*, p. 362 (footnote omitted).

[20] *Ibid.*, p. 365.

[21] ICRC, *Commentary on the Additional Protocols*, p. 695.

[22] *Ibid.*, p. 685.

The second requirement in the principle of proportionality is that the foreseeable injury to civilians and damage to civilian objects should not be disproportionate, that is, "excessive" in comparison to the expected "concrete and definite military advantage." Excessive damage is also a relative concept. For instance, the presence of a soldier on leave cannot serve as a justification for destroying the entire village. If the destruction of a bridge is of paramount importance for the occupation of a strategic zone, "it is understood that some houses may be hit, but not that a whole urban area be levelled." There is never a justification for excessive civilian casualties, no matter how valuable the military target.

Indiscriminate attacks are defined in Protocol I, Article 51 (4), as:

> a) those which are not directed at a specific military objective;
> b) those which employ a method or means of combat which cannot be directed at a specific military objective; or
> c) those which employ a method or means of combat the effects of which cannot be limited as required by this Protocol; and consequently, in each such case, are of a nature to strike military objectives and civilians or civilian objects without distinction.

PROTECTION OF CIVILIANS FROM DISPLACEMENT FOR REASONS RELATED TO THE CONFLICT

There are only two exceptions to the prohibition from displacement, for war-related reasons, of civilians: their security or imperative military reasons. Article 17 of Protocol II states:

> 1. The displacement of the civilian population shall not be ordered for reasons related to the conflict unless the security of the civilians involved or imperative military reasons so demand. Should such displacements have to be carried out, all possible measures shall be taken in order that the civilian population may be received under satisfactory conditions of shelter, hygiene, health, safety and nutrition.

The term "imperative military reasons" usually refers to evacuation because of imminent military operations. A provisional measure of evacuation is appropriate if an area is in danger as a result of military operations or is liable to be subjected to intense bombing. It may also be permitted when the presence of protected persons in an area hampers military operations. The prompt return of the evacuees to their homes is required as soon as hostilities in the area have ceased. The evacuating authority bears the burden of proving that its forcible relocation conforms to these conditions.

Displacement or capture of civilians solely to deny a social base to the enemy has nothing to do with the security of the civilians. Nor is it justified by "imperative military reasons," which require "the most meticulous assessment of the circumstances"[23] because such reasons are capable of abuse. One authority has stated: "Clearly, imperative military reasons cannot be justified by political motives. For example, it would be prohibited to move a population in order to exercise more effective control over a dissident ethnic group."[24]

Mass relocation or displacement of civilians for the purpose of denying a willing social base to the opposing force is prohibited since it is a political motive as described above. Even if the government were to show that the displacement were necessary, it still has the independent obligation to take "all possible measures" to receive the civilian population "under satisfactory conditions of shelter, hygiene, health, safety, and nutrition."

STARVATION OF CIVILIANS AS A METHOD OF COMBAT

Starvation of civilians as a method of combat has become illegal as a matter of customary law, as reflected in Protocol II:

> Article 14 -- Protection of objects indispensable to the survival of the civilian population
>
> Starvation of civilians as a method of combat is prohibited. It is prohibited to attack, destroy, remove or render useless, for that purpose, objects indispensable to the survival of the civilian population, such as foodstuffs, agricultural areas for the production of foodstuffs, crops, livestock, drinking water installations and supplies and irrigation works.

---

[23] *Ibid.*, p. 1472.

[24] *Ibid.*

Starvation is also prohibited as "a weapon to annihilate or weaken the population." Using starvation as a method of warfare does not mean that the population has to reach the point of starving to death before a violation can be proved. What is forbidden is deliberately "causing the population to suffer hunger, particularly by depriving it of sources of food or of supplies." This prohibition "is a rule from which no derogation may be made."[25] No exception can be made for imperative military necessity, for instance.

Article 14 lists the most usual ways in which starvation is brought about. Specific protection is extended to "objects indispensable to the survival of the civilian population," and a non-exhaustive list of such objects follows: "foodstuffs, agricultural areas for the production of foodstuffs, crops, livestock, drinking water installations and supplies and irrigation works." The article prohibits taking certain destructive actions aimed at these essential supplies, and describes these actions with verbs which are meant to cover all eventualities: "attack, destroy, remove or render useless." The textual reference to "objects indispensable to the survival of the civilian population" does not distinguish between objects intended for the armed forces and those intended for civilians. Except in the case of supplies specifically intended as provisions for combatants, it is prohibited to destroy or attack objects indispensable for survival, even if the adversary may benefit from them. The prohibition would be meaningless if one could invoke the argument that members of the government's armed forces or armed opposition might make use of the objects in question.[26]

Attacks on objects used "in direct support of military action" are permissible, however, even if these objects are civilian foodstuffs and other objects protected under Article 14. The exception is limited to the immediate zone of actual armed engagements, as is obvious from the examples provided of military objects used in direct support of military action: "bombarding a food-producing area to prevent the army from advancing through it, or attacking a food-storage barn which is being used by the enemy for cover or as an arms depot, etc."[27]

---

[25] *Ibid.*, p. 1456.

[26] *Ibid.*, p. 1458-59.

[27] *Ibid.*, p. 657. *New Rules* gives the following examples of direct support: "an irrigation canal used as part of a defensive position, a water tower used as an observation post, or a cornfield used as cover for the infiltration of an attacking force." Bothe, *New Rules for Victims of Armed Conflict*, p. 341.

The provisions of Protocol I, Article 54 are also useful as a guideline to the narrowness of the permissible means and methods of attack on foodstuffs.[28] Like Article 14 of Protocol II, Article 54 of Protocol I permits attacks on military food supplies. It specifically limits such attacks to those directed at foodstuffs intended for the sole use of the enemy's armed forces. This means "supplies already in the hands of the adverse party's armed forces because it is only at that point that one could know that they are intended for use only for the members of the enemy's armed forces."[29] Even then, the attacker cannot destroy foodstuffs "in the military supply system intended for the sustenance of prisoners of war, the civilian population of occupied territory or persons classified as civilians serving with, or accompanying, the armed forces."[30]

Proof of Intention to Starve Civilians

Under Article 14, what is forbidden are actions taken with the intention of using starvation as a method or weapon to attack the civilian population. Such an intention may not be easy to prove and most armies will not admit this intention. Proof does not rest solely on the attacker's own admissions, however. Intention may be inferred from the totality of the circumstances of the military campaign. Particularly relevant to assessment of intention is the effort the attacker makes to comply with the duties to distinguish between civilians and military targets and to avoid harming civilians and the civilian economy by choosing means of attack less harmful to civilians. If the attacker does not comply with these duties, and food shortages result, an intention to attack civilians by starvation may be inferred.

The more sweeping and indiscriminate the measures taken which result in food shortages, when other less restrictive means of combat are available, the more likely the real intention is to attack the civilian population by causing it food deprivation. For instance, an attacker who conducts a scorched earth campaign in enemy territory and destroys all or most sources of food may be deemed to have an intention of attacking by starvation the civilian population living in enemy territory. The attacker may not claim ignorance of the effects

---

[28] Article 54 of Protocol I is parallel, for international armed conflicts, to Article 14 of Protocol II in its prohibition on starvation of civilians as a method of warfare.

[29] Bothe, *New Rules for Victims of Armed Conflict*, p. 340.

[30] *Ibid.*, pp. 340-41.

upon civilians of such a scorched earth campaign, since these effects are a matter of common knowledge and publicity. In particular, relief organizations, both domestic and international, usually sound the alarm of food shortages occurring during conflicts in order to bring pressure on the parties to permit access for food delivery and to raise money for their complex and costly operations.

The true intentions of the attacker also must be judged by the effort he makes to take prompt remedies, such as permitting relief convoys to reach the needy or itself supplying food to remedy civilian hunger. An attacker who fails to make adequate provision for the affected civilian population, who blocks access to those who would do so, or who refuses to permit civilian evacuation in times of food shortage, may be deemed to have the intention to starve that civilian population.

SIEGES

Proportionality is an important principle in the context of sieges and other methods of war directed at combatants operating among civilians. While starvation of the civilian population is forbidden, starvation of combatants remains a permitted method of combat, as in siege warfare or blockades.[31]

A blockade consists of disrupting the maritime trade of a country; a siege consists of encircling an enemy location, cutting off those inside from any communication in order to bring about their surrender.[32]

Siege is the oldest form of total war, in which civilians have been attacked along with soldiers, or in order to reach soldiers. A siege may occur when an army takes refuge inside city walls, or when the inhabitants of a threatened city seek the most immediate form of military protection and agree to be garrisoned.[33] Both blockades and sieges are theoretically aimed at

---

[31] ICRC, *Commentary on the Additional Protocols*, p. 1457.

[32] *Ibid.*, p. 1457.

[33] Michael Walzer, *Just and Unjust Wars* (New York: Basic Books, 1977), p. 160.

preventing military materiel from reaching the combatants. Both are considered low-cost alternatives to frontal assaults.[34]

Under the rule of proportionality and the duty to distinguish civilians from combatants, besieging forces may not close their eyes to the effect upon civilians of a food blockade or siege. It is well recognized that, in reality, "in case of shortages occasioned by armed conflict,the highest priority of available sustenance materials is assigned to combatants."[35] In other words, "Fed last, and only with the army's surplus [civilians] die first. More civilians died in the siege of Leningrad than in the modernist infernos of Hamburg, Dresden, Tokyo, Hiroshima and Nagasaki, taken together."[36] The besieging forces therefore are deemed to know that, in any besieged area where civilians as well as combatants are present, the civilians will suffer food shortage long before the combatants.

Historically, sieges therefore have been used as weapons to bring pressure by suffering civilians on the military leadership.
When a city is encircled and deprived of food, the attackers do not operate in the expectation that the garrison will hold out until the individual soldiers, like Josephus' old men, drop dead in the streets. Deaths among the ordinary inhabitants of the city are expected to force the hand of the civilian or military leadership. The goal is surrender; the means is not the defeat of the enemy army, but the fearful spectacle of the civilian dead.[37]

One authority notes that soldiers "are under an obligation to help civilians leave the scene of a battle." In the case of a siege, "it is only when they fulfill this obligation that the battle itself is morally possible. But is it still militarily possible? Once free exit has been offered, and been accepted by a significant number of people, the besieging army is placed under a certain

---

[34] One historian notes that "the capture of cities is often an important military objective—in the age of the city-state, it was the ultimate objective—and, frontal assault failing, the siege is the only remaining means to success. In fact, however, it is not even necessary that a frontal assault fail before a siege is thought justifiable. Sitting and waiting is far less costly to the besieged army than attacking, and such calculations are permitted by the principle of military necessity." *Ibid.*, p. 169.

[35] Bothe, *New Rules for Victims of Armed Conflicts,* p. 680.

[36] Walzer, *Just and Unjust Wars*, p. 160.

[37] *Ibid.*

handicap. The city's food supply will now last so much longer. It is precisely this handicap that siege commanders have in the past refused to accept."[38]

Under the prohibition on starving the civilian population as a method of combat, sieges are a form of starvation by omission. The ICRC notes that:

> Starvation can also result from an omission. To deliberately decide not to take measures to supply the population with objects indispensable for its survival in a way would become a method of combat by default, and would be prohibited under this rule.[39]

It is therefore incumbent upon the attackers, in sieges and blockades as well as in other methods of combat, to take actions to ameliorate the effects upon civilians. The Protocols suggest various options, among them permitting relief supplies to the civilian population.[40] Failure to take action to relieve the threat of civilian starvation leads directly to the inference that the intention of the besieging forces is to starve civilians.

RECRUITMENT OF CHILD SOLDIERS

Military recruitment of those under the age of fifteen is forbidden.[41]

---

[38] *Ibid.*, pp. 169-70.

[39] ICRC, *Commentary on the Additional Protocols*, p. 1458.

[40] See Protocol I, Articles 68-71.

[41] Protocol II, Article 4 (3) provides:
Children shall be provided with the care and aid they require, and in particular:

(a) they shall receive an education, including religious and moral education, in keeping with the wishes of their parents or, in the absence of parents, of those responsible for their care,
(b) all appropriate steps shall be taken to facilitate the reunion of families temporarily separated;
(c) children who have not attained the age of fifteen years shall neither be recruited in the armed forces or groups nor allowed to take part in hostilities;

This principle also prohibits accepting voluntary enlistment. A child should not be allowed to take part in hostilities, that is, to participate in military operations including gathering information, transmitting orders, transporting orders, transporting ammunition and foodstuffs, or acts of sabotage.[42] The reason for applying such special rules for children in warfare is obvious: "Children are particularly vulnerable; they require privileged treatment in comparison with the rest of the civilian population."[43]

In addition to the rules of war, other authoritative guidance is provided by the Convention on the Rights of the Child.[44] The provisions of Protocol II are echoed in Article 38 (2) of the Convention on the Rights of the Child, stating that the parties "shall take all feasible measures to ensure that persons who have not attained the age of fifteen years do not take a direct part in hostilities." The parties to the Convention also agreed that in "recruiting among those persons who have attained the age of fifteen years but who have not attained the age of eighteen years, [we] shall endeavor to give priority to those who are oldest."[45] The Convention goes on to state in Article 9 as a matter of principle that a child shall not be separated from his or her parents against their will except where such separation is deemed necessary in the best interests of

---

(d) the special protection provided by the Article to children who had not attained the age of fifteen years shall remain applicable to them if they take a direct part in hostilities despite the provisions of sub-paragraph (c) and are captured;

(e)measures shall be taken, if necessary, and whenever possible with the consent of their parents or persons who by law or custom are primarily responsible for their care, to remove children temporarily from the area in which hostilities are taking place to a safer area within the country and ensure that they are accompanied by persons responsible for their safety and well-being.

[42] ICRC, *Commentary on the Additional Protocols*, p. 1380.

[43] *Ibid.*, p. 1377.

[44] Angola ratified this Convention on May 12, 1990. Under the Convention, Angola is obligated to submit periodic reports. One was due on March 1, 1992 and as of August 12, 1994, it had not been submitted. This convention applies to State Parties and makes no mention of rebel groups, but does provide authoritative guidance for interpreting customary international humanitarian law applicable to rebels.

[45] Convention on the Rights of the Child, art. 38(2).

the child after judicial review. Forced recruitment of children violates these principles as well as the rules of war.

Although it has not yet come into effect, the African Convention on the Rights and the Welfare of the Child prohibits recruitment of those under eighteen years of age.[46]

---

[46] African Charter on the Rights and Welfare of the Child, CAB/LEG/153/Rev.2, Organization of African Unity, Addis Ababa, Ethiopia. The Charter defines "child" as below eighteen years of age. The Charter states at Article 22 (2): "States Parties to the present Charter shall take all necessary measures to ensure that no child shall take a direct part in hostilities and refrain in particular from recruiting any child."

IX. RECOMMENDATIONS

Angolan Government

Human Rights Watch calls on the Angolan government to:

● Respect international humanitarian and human rights law, particularly the prohibitions on targeting civilians, indiscriminate bombardment, and destruction or looting of civilian property;

● Cease using aerial bombardment against urban areas and other zones where bombs cannot be reasonably aimed at military objectives;

● Stop using weapons particularly harmful to the civilian population, such as antipersonnel landmines and cluster bombs;

● Prohibit summary executions and torture, and punish those responsible for such acts;

● Stop recruitment of minors and use of child soldiers; refrain from seizing those under the age of eighteen for military service or permitting them to participate in hostilities;

● Halt the seizure by troops and officials of food and non-food items from the civilian population that expose civilians to the threat of death through starvation, disease, or exposure;

● Permit the International Committee of the Red Cross to visit persons detained in connection with the conflict, according to its specific criteria.

UNITA

Human Rights Watch calls on UNITA to:

● Respect international humanitarian law, particularly the prohibitions on targeting civilians, indiscriminate bombardment, and destruction or looting of civilian property;

- Cease using starvation as a method of combat;

- Stop indiscriminate shelling of besieged cities;

- Stop attacking humanitarian relief operations;

- Stop using weapons particularly harmful to the civilian population, particularly antipersonnel landmines;

- Prohibit summary executions and torture, and punish those responsible for such acts;

- Refrain from involuntary recruitment;

- Stop recruitment of minors and use of child soldiers; refrain from seizing those under the age of eighteen for military service or permitting them to participate in hostilities;

- Stop forced portering;

- Facilitate voluntary family reunification;

- Permit freedom of movement;

- Halt the seizure by soldiers and officials of food and non-food items from the civilian population that expose civilians to the threat of death through starvation, disease, or exposure;

- Permit the International Committee of the Red Cross to visit persons detained in connection with the conflict, according to its specific criteria;

- Cooperate with relief efforts and human rights monitors and educators, and facilitate their access to all parts of the country.

United Nations

Human Rights Watch recommends that the U.N. Security Council:

•   Institute an arms embargo on Angola, applicable to both the government and UNITA;

•   Strongly encourage all member states to submit information on past weapons exports to Angola to the U.N. Register on Conventional Arms;

•   Deploy full-time U.N. monitors at Zaire's Ndjili international airport to tighten U.N. sanctions against UNITA;

•   Authorize a contingent of full-time U.N. human rights monitors to observe, investigate, bring to the attention of the responsible authorities, and make public violations of international humanitarian law and internationally recognized human rights principles by all parties; the monitors should have access to all parts of Angola and some should be based in locations well-placed for access to the changing fronts of the conflict; when the U.N. monitors obtain information, it should be made highly transparent, so that it is evident, as quickly as possible, when infringements have been committed and by whom;

•   Draft a ceasefire agreement so that its terms do not reward military aggression and violations of the laws of war since the breaking of the Bicesse Accords, and ensure that human rights are explicitly to be protected by the implementation mechanisms of the agreement;

•   Once a peace agreement is signed, expand the deployment of human rights monitors and launch a civilian-directed and -staffed program of human rights education across the country irrespective of party, creed or ethnic origin.

The Observing Troika (Portugal, Russia, United States)

Human Rights Watch recommends that Portugal, Russia and the U.S. as mediators in the peace process should:

•   Impose immediate national arms embargoes, applicable to both the Angolan government and UNITA;

•   Release details immediately on any weapons sales to any party in Angola since the Triple Zero clause was lifted;

•   Maintain pressure on the Angolan government and particularly UNITA to respect human rights and humanitarian law and permit access to relief operations;

•   Support the creation of a full-time U.N. human rights monitoring team.

South African, Zairian, and Other Governments in the Region

Human Rights Watch calls on the South African, Zairian, and other governments in the region to:

•   Assist the U.N. in all its attempts to monitor UNITA sanction-busting;

•   Stop mercenary support which contributes to violations of the laws of war in Angola;

•   In particular, the government of Zaire should take all measures to stop the use of Zaire as a conduit for illegal arms trade, and should not allow UNITA to maintain rear bases in Zairian border areas.

APPENDIX: SUMÁRIO EM PORTUGUÉS

Angola mergulhou-se de novo na guerra semanas após a realização das primeiras eleições gerais no país, em setembro de 1992. Embora não seja possível calcular com precisão o custo humano do recomeço da guerra em Angola, de acordo com estimativas das Nações Unidas, em meados de 1993, cerca de 1000 pessoas morriam diariamente devido ao conflito, à fome e à doenca, a maior percentagem mundial de mortes registadas na altura devido à guerra. Em outubro de 1993 foram noticiadas, apenas na cidade de Malanje, as mortes de 250 crianças por dia. [1] Em setembro de 1994, o Secretário-Geral das Nações Unidas declarou haver um aumento de 10 por cento no número de pessoas seriamente afectadas pela guerra desde fevereiro de 1994, e que perto de 3,7 milhões de angolanos, na sua maioria deslocados e pessoas afectadas pelo conflito, precisavam de medicamentos, vacinas e ajuda alimentar. [2]

Para além das chocantes percentagens de mortes e da destruição, a guerra angolana é significativa devido às violações generalizadas e sistemáticas das leis de guerra, tanto por parte do governo do Movimento Popular de Libertação de Angola (MPLA) como dos rebeldes da União Nacional para a Independência Total de Angola (UNITA). Os bombardeamentos indiscriminados da UNITA de cidades sitiadas e afectadas pela fome, em particular, provocaram a destruição em massa de propriedades e um número indeterminado de mortes de civis. Os bombardeamentos indiscriminados levados a cabo pelo governo resultaram igualmente em pesadas baixas civis. Conforme sublinhou um especialista em África do Departamento de Defesa dos Estados Unidos, "este tipo de guerra recai sobretudo, com crueldade e de forma desproporcional, na população, a qual é apanhada no meio das partes beligerantes."[3] Se o custo

---

[1] As mortes de crianças terão diminuído para 26 por dia em janeiro de 1994. Veja, *Angola in Strife*, Situation Report No. 6, U.S. Agency for International Development, 7 de abril de 1994.

[2] Conselho de Segurança das Nações Unidas, "Report of the Secretary-General on the United Nations Angola Verification Mission," Setembro 1994.

[3] James Woods, Sub-Secretário da Defesa para Assuntos Africanos, no seu discurso "The Quest for Peace in Angola" pronunciado perante o Subcomité da África do Comité das Relações Externas da Câmara dos Representantes, (Washington: U.S. Government Printing Office), Novembro 16, 1993, p.7. James Woods previa que as baixas militares

humano da guerra em Angola é extraordinário, tambem o é a falta de atenção internacional. O conflito angolano passou a ter a alcunha da "guerra esquecida".

Este relatório documenta as violações das leis de guerra e o fluxo de armamento que alimenta essas violações, em Angola, desde as eleições de 1992. As eleições foram a meta do fracassado tratado de paz, os Acordos de Bicesse, assinados em Portugal no dia 31 de maio de 1991 pelo governo do MPLA e a UNITA. Os acordos continham a cláusula intitulada de "Triplo Zero" que proibia a ambas as partes adquirir novos fornecimentos de armas. Durante o período de transição que culminou com as eleições de 1992, o governo e a UNITA nao cumpriram com a sua obrigação de desmobilizar os soldados. Em vez disso, ambos aparentemente mantiveram exércitos secretos, e o governo criou uma nova força policial paramilitar, os "Ninjas". A Organização das Nações Unidas, contando com um mandato reduzido e recursos imensamente inadequados, foi ineficaz durante esse período, e manteve-se virtualmente silenciosa quanto a ocorrência de abusos dos direitos humanos.

Após a vitória eleitoral do MPLA, a UNITA rejeitou os resultados e lançou uma ofensiva militar que rapidamente escalou para o retorno da guerra civil alargada em Angola, continuando a registar-se até ao presente violentos combates no país.

A renovação do conflito, os abusos dos direitos humanos e as violações das leis de guerra estão a ser alimentados por novos fluxos de armas que entram no país. Há evidência de que o governo recebeu carregamentos de armas por via marítima em 1991 e 1992, em violação dos Acordos de Bicesse, provenientes sobretudo da Rússia e do Brasil. Com o recomeço da guerra em Angola, o governo revogou o embargo de armas Triplo Zero para de seguida se lançar desenfreadamente no mercado internacional de armas. Entre 1993 e 1994 o governo angolano dispendeu mais de 3,5 bilhões de dólares na compra de armamento. A compra de armas atingiu proporções recordes, chegando mesmo a ultrapassar os níveis extraordinários de meados dos anos 80, quando a União Soviética fornecia armas a Angola como a sua parte da guerra indirecta das superpotências. O governo de Angola tem sido nos últimos dois anos, sem qualquer dúvida, o maior comprador de armas da África sub-saariana. Com as gigantescas importações de armas, o governo parece estar a sacrificar o seu futuro económico. Alguns analistas acreditam que Angola tenha já empenhado a receita dos próximos 7 anos de produção petrolífera para financiar a compra

---

constituíam, "apenas um total de alguns milhares", enquanto que o número de mortes de civis poderia ter atingido o meio milhão. Ibid.

de armas, apesar de previsões de que as suas reservas de petróleo estarão esgotadas em 15 anos.

O governo continua a comprar todo o tipo de armamentos, desde armas ligeiras e munições a tanques e aviões-caça, incluindo sistemas avançados nunca antes vistos em Angola, tais como os tanques T-72. O governo compra armas de origem diversa, como seja da Europa, África, Ásia e América Latina, sendo, no entanto, grande parte dos armamentos comprados através de comerciantes internacionais de armas. A maior parte dos negócios de compra de armas realiza-se secretamente, ou através de subterfúgios; muitas das transacções envolvem o uso de documentação falsa, ou envolvem entidades governamentais e privadas múltiplas. A Rússia terá herdado da antiga União Soviética o título de maior fornecedor de armas a Angola. Entre outros países aparentemente envolvidos em armar o governo de Angola incluem-se : o Brasil, a Ucrânia, a Bulgária, o Uzbequistão, a Coreia do Norte, Portugal e Espanha. Portugal e a Rússia actuaram de forma irresponsável ao minimizarem o seu papel de membros oficiais da "Troika de Observadores" do processo de paz.

Uma firma privada sul-africana de "consultas sobre segurança", a Executive Outcomes, terá fornecido pessoal armado para assistir tanto as forças da UNITA como do governo, e possuirá actualmente um contracto com o governo angolano na ordem de milhões de dólares.

A UNITA compra grandes quantidades de armamento de fontes estrangeiras. Essas aquisições violam tanto os Acordos de Bicesse de 1991 como o embargo internacional de armas e de petróleo impostos contra a UNITA pelo Conselho de Segurança das Nações Unidas em setembro de 1993. A UNITA tem sido eficaz em "contrariar as sanções" através dos países vizinhos, a África do Sul, em especial, a Namíbia e o Zaire. Ao que parece, a UNITA obtem grande parte das suas armas de fontes privadas e não de governos estrangeiros, apesar de haver alguma prova de que a Rússia, o Zaire e outros países lhe tenham fornecido armas. O Zaire tornou-se a maior fonte de apoio à UNITA. A UNITA usa o Zaire como uma área de trânsito e via de venda de diamantes e transferências de armas. A UNITA mantem ainda várias bases de retaguarda no Zaire e recebe apoio operacional de tropas zairenses.

A UNITA financia a sua campanha militar, incluindo a importação ilegal de armas, com a riqueza diamantífera de Angola. O cartel de diamantes De Beers e outros comerciantes internacionais compram diamantes provenientes de minas, das áreas controladas pela UNITA, exploradas em violação da lei angolana. A maior parte dos diamantes são transportados ilegalmente através da fronteira do sul do Zaire e, em menor quantidade, através da fronteira da Zâmbia. De Beers admite ter gasto 500 milhões de dólares na compra, legal e ilegal, de diamantes de Angola em 1992. O dinheiro do comércio de diamante substitui a ajuda que a UNITA recebia anteriormente dos Estados Unidos e da África do Sul. A ajuda secreta dos Estados Unidos a UNITA totalizou cerca de 250 milhões de dólares entre 1986 e 1991.

O governo angolano é responsável por extensos abusos e violações das leis de guerra desde as eleições de setembro de 1992, entre os quais se incluem:

- o bombardeamento aéreo indiscriminado de centros populacionais;
- o uso da tortura, desaparecimentos e execuções sumárias, especialmente contra suspeitos apoiantes da UNITA nas áreas urbanas;
- mortes de civis e pilhagem durante operações militares;
- restrições nas operações humanitárias das agências internacionais e das Nações Unidas, e impunidade de oficiais militares e outros que vendem alimentos de origem humanitária para fins lucrativos;
- o recrutamento militar obrigatório e de pessoal menor;
- a deslocação forçada da população civil; e
- condições desumanas e cruéis nas prisões.

As forças governamentais, e grupos civis armados pelo governo, mataram e torturaram milhares de suspeitos apoiantes da UNITA - ou seja, civis não-combatentes - entre outubro de 1992 e janeiro de 1993 numa operação de limpeza levada a cabo nas cidades após o recomeço da guerra. Entre 1993 e 1994, milhares de outros civis foram mortos ou feridos durante bombardeamentos indiscriminados de centros populacionais de zonas controladas pela UNITA.

A UNITA perpetrou violações sistemáticas e atrozes das leis de guerra, entre as quais:

- o bombardeamento indiscriminado de cidades sitiadas;
- a execução sumária e tortura;
- tentativas de causar a fome junto da população civil ao atacar as operações humanitárias internacionais, ao colocar minas nas trilhas e no campo, ao sabotar meios de transporte terrestres, ao capturar e matar camponeses;
- a mutilação de mortos;

• o rapto de civis, incluindo mulheres e crianças, para fins de recrutamento militar forçado, tratando-os por vezes como escravos;

• o recrutamento militar obrigatório e de pessoal menor, a recusa de permitir que menores não acompanhados se reúnam voluntariamente com as suas famílias;

• o sequestro de reféns estrangeiros, alguns dos quais tendo sido usados como "escudo humano";

• a restrição na movimentação de civis nas áreas sob sua ocupação; a confiscação dos seus alimentos e a obrigatoriedade de trabalharem sem remuneração, e

• condições desumanas e cruéis nas prisões.

A UNITA efectuou o cerco de vários centros citadinos e cidades, o Huambo e o Kuito, em especial. A UNITA bombardeou ambas as cidades com cerca de 1000 granadas diárias. Estimativas colocam em 10 mil o número de pessoas, muitas das quais civis, que morreram na batalha para a captura de Huambo. Quando tomou posse de Huambo, a UNITA matou brutalmente muitos civis que ficaram na cidade ou que se encontravam em trânsito nas estradas de saída da cidade. Acredita-se que 15 mil pessoas tenham morrido durante os nove meses de cerco de Kuito que completamente devastou a cidade. Os cercos da UNITA provocaram fome em larga escala junto da população civil, especialmente em Kuito e Malanje. Os ataques da UNITA contra as operações humanitárias foram numerosas e bem documentadas.

A guerra das minas intensificou-se desde que recomeçaram as hostilidades, com milhares de novas minas a serem colocadas tanto pelo governo como pela UNITA com o objectivo de: obstruir estradas e pontes, rodear as cidades sitiadas com círculos de minas de largura atingindo até 3 kilometros, e para impedir o cultivo de terras. De acordo com estimativas, entre 9 a 15 milhões de minas foram colocadas em todo o país. Estimativas da ONU prevêm que o número de mutilados em Angola em 1994 atingirá os 70 mil.

Iniciativas de mediação da ONU e de outras entidades foram muitas vezes ignoradas tanto pela intransigência da UNITA como do governo do MPLA, e ainda pelas tentativas de ambas as partes em usar as negociações para obter vantagens no campo da batalha. A política dos Estados Unidos para Angola mudou pouco em relação ao que era na fase final da administração Bush, apesar de ter havido o reconhecimento oficial do governo de Angola. A antiga política de armar a UNITA foi substituída por iniciativas políticas destinadas a fazer avançar o processo de paz. Aparentemente, Angola não constitui grande prioridade para a política externa dos Estados Unidos. A administração Clinton tem permanecido em grande parte silenciosa quanto aos abusos dos direitos humanos e violações das leis de guerra em Angola.

PRINCIPAIS RECOMENDAÇÕES

A Human Rights Watch exorta o governo angolano a respeitar as leis humanitárias internacionais assim como os direitos humanos, especialmente as proibições: de atacar civis, de levar a cabo bombardeamentos indiscriminados e a destruição e pilhagem de propriedade civil. O governo deveria pôr termo ao uso de armas especialmente perigosas para a população civil, tais como as minas terrestres e as bombas de fragmentação. O governo deveria proibir a realização de execuções sumárias assim como da tortura e punir os responsáveis por tais actos. O governo deveria impedir que as tropas confisquem alimentos ou outros suprimentos não alimentares da população civil por forma a ameaçar a vida de civis através da fome, doença, e vulnerabilidade. O governo deve pôr termo ao uso de soldados menores de idade e ao recrutamento involuntário. O governo deveria permitir ao Comité Internacional da Cruz Vermelha visitar pessoas detidas devido ao conflito.

A Human Rights Watch exorta a UNITA a respeitar a lei humanitária internacional, em particular as proibições: de ataques a civis, de bombardeamentos indiscriminados e de destruição e pilhagem de propriedade civil. A UNITA deveria cessar imediatamente: de usar a fome como método de combate, de bombardear indiscriminadamente as cidades e de atacar as operações humanitárias. A UNITA deveria pôr termo ao uso de armas especialmente perigosas para a população civil, tais como as minas contra a vida humana. A UNITA deveria proibir a realização de execuções sumárias e da tortura, e punir as pessoas responsáveis por esses actos. A UNITA deveria pôr termo ao uso de soldados menores de idade e o recrutamento involuntário e deveria deixar de forçar as pessoas a transportarem abastecimentos a pé. A UNITA deveria permitir a liberdade de movimento e facilitar a reunião de familiares. A UNITA deveria impedir que as suas tropas confisquem alimentos ou outros suprimentos não alimentares da população civil por forma a ameaçar a vida de civis através da fome, doença, e vulnerabilidade. A UNITA deveria permitir à Cruz Vermelha Internacional visitar pessoas detidas em consequência do conflito. A UNITA deveria cooperar com os esforços humanitários e com os inspectores e educadores dos direitos humanos, e facilitar o seu acesso a todas as partes do país.

Human Rights Watch recomenda que o Conselho de Segurança das Nações Unidas imponha um embargo de armas a Angola, aplicável tanto ao governo como a UNITA. Os estados membros das Nações Unidas deveriam fornecer informação completa ao Registo de Armas Convencionais das Nações Unidas sobre as exportações de armas efectuadas no passado a Angola. A ONU deveria estacionar inspectores no aeroporto internacional de Ndjili no Zaire com o objectivo de manter um controle mais rígido das sanções das Nações Unidas contra a UNITA. A ONU deveria autorizar a formação de uma equipa completa de inspectores, especialistas em direitos humanos, para observar, investigar e levar casos de infracção a atenção das entidades competentes e divulgar os abusos dos direitos humanos e violações das leis humanitárias por ambas as partes. Os inspectores deveriam ter acesso a todas as partes de Angola e alguns deveriam ficar baseados em áreas bem localizadas a fim de ter fácil acesso às variadas frentes do conflito.

A ONU deveria elaborar um projecto de acordo de cessar-fogo que não gratifique a agressão militar e violações das leis de guerra desde que foram violados os acordos de Bicesse. Os direitos humanos terão que ser protegidos nos termos do acordo. Após a assinatura de um acordo de paz, a ONU deveria expandir o estacionamento de inspectores e lançar um programa de educação das populações civis sobre os direitos humanos dirigido pelos próprios civis em todo o país sem considerações partidárias, de crença ou origem étnica.

Human Rights Watch recomenda a Portugal, a Rússia e aos Estados Unidos, no seu papel de mediadores oficiais do processo de paz, a imporem de imediato um embargo de armas a nível nacional, e a fornecerem detalhes sobre qualquer venda de armas ou outro tipo de assistência militar a qualquer das partes no conflito de Angola, desde a assinatura dos Acordos de Bicesse em 1991. Esses observadores deveriam pressionar o governo angolano e a UNITA, em especial, a respeitarem os direitos humanos e a lei internacional humanitária e a permitirem acesso às operações humanitárias. Esses países deveriam apoiar a criação de uma equipa permanente de verificação dos direitos humanos da ONU.

Human Rights Watch apela aos presidentes sul-africano e zairense, assim como aos outros chefes de estado regionais, a assistirem a ONU nas suas tentativas de verificação e de impedir a UNITA de contrariar as sanções. Esses governos deveriam proibir qualquer apoio mercenário que contribua para a violação das leis de guerra. O governo do Zaire deveria tomar todas as medidas para pôr termo ao uso do território zairense como via de contrabando de armas e não permitir que a UNITA mantenha bases de retaguarda no interior das fronteiras zairenses.